P9-DNM-143

More praise for
When Society Becomes an Addict

"Another breakthrough book by Anne Wilson Schaef. This time, with startling honesty, she takes us to the heart and soul of our addictions as a society and as individuals."
—Dr. Ken Druck, author of *The Secrets Men Keep*

"This is an antidote to the systemic poisons that threaten to overwhelm us. A much-needed reflection during these times when the evening news is filled with drug overdoses, family violence, workaholism, cults, faddish cravings, and compulsive, driven politics. . . . *When Society Becomes an Addict* moves the reader again and again to 'Aha, yes!' recognitions of our deeply human vulnerability to addiction. . . . [It] can help us to reform ourselves, our corporate cultures, and our public policies. . . . This important book provides a 'grid' on which we can plot, observe our behavior, and begin the task of reshaping this lethal 'game' that drives our culture."
—Madonna Kolbenschlag, author of *Kiss Sleeping Beauty Good-Bye*

"Anne Wilson Schaef not only confronts us with a new model for understanding ourselves and our world in a new way, but she also offers help in shedding addict patterns of behavior in both our individual and societal lives."
—Robert McAfee Brown

"Anne Wilson Schaef has a brilliant talent for seeing the connections in complex systems of human behavior and interpreting those patterns in the language of everyday experience. . . . In this book she breaks down the barriers between the personal and the political and shows the parallels between patterns of pathological behavior in private addiction and those that pervade our public, social, and political life."
—Rosemary Radford Ruether, author of *Sexism and God-Talk*

"Anne Wilson Schaef has profoundly explicated the evolutionary devastation we as a human family are currently experiencing in addictive patterns of living that are devoid of spiritual significance. . . . Here is a landmark work that gives us clarity and specific guidelines about the process of 'whole-system recovery.' "

—Jacquelyn Small, author of *Transformers,*
the Therapists of the Future

"In *Women's Reality,* Anne Wilson Schaef did an amazing job of bringing together much feminist thinking. She expanded our consciousness and brought us home to our own ground of being. In her latest work, *When Society Becomes an Addict,* Schaef moves beyond the homecoming celebration and makes new space for all to grow."

—Dagmar Celeste, First Lady of Ohio

"Schaef draws together diverse insights—from psychotherapy, social criticism, and the 'people experience' of groups such as Alcoholics Anonymous and Gamblers Anonymous—to show how a different life is possible, how healing can happen, and how a different world can be shaped."

—Elizabeth Dodson Gray, author of *Green Paradise Lost*
and *Patriarchy As a Conceptual Trap*

"Anne Wilson Schaef is a brilliant observer of the 'layers of behavior' that many of us have not yet seen. Her new book is a breakthrough into new layers of 'seeing and naming.' "

—Linda L. Moore, psychologist and author

"We read with great pleasure *When Society Becomes an Addict* by Anne Wilson Schaef. She clearly answers questions we have all known but have been afraid to ask. As members of a whole family system that opted for recovery, we can only say thank you for affirming our own lives and beliefs."

—Jess Lair and Jacqueline Lair, authors of *I Don't Know Where I'm*
Going—But I Sure Ain't Lost

"Our addictions personally and culturally are killing us. At last someone has had the wisdom and the courage to name our disease —and to offer some guidelines for recovery. Americans individually and collectively would do well to heed Anne Wilson Schaef's message."

—Nancy A. Hardesty, author of *All We're Meant to Be:*
Biblical Feminism Today

WHEN SOCIETY BECOMES AN ADDICT

WHEN SOCIETY BECOMES AN ADDICT

Anne Wilson Schaef

Harper & Row, Publishers, San Francisco

Cambridge, Hagerstown, New York, Philadelphia, Washington
London, Mexico City, São Paulo, Singapore, Sydney

WHEN SOCIETY BECOMES AN ADDICT. Copyright © 1987 by Anne Wilson Schaef. All rights reserved. Printed in the United States of America. No part of this book may be used or reproduced in any manner whatsoever without written permission except in the case of brief quotations embodied in critical articles and reviews. For information address Harper & Row, Publishers, Inc., 10 East 53rd Street, New York, NY 10022. Published simultaneously in Canada by Fitzhenry & Whiteside, Limited, Toronto.

FIRST HARPER & ROW PAPERBACK EDITION PUBLISHED IN 1988.

Library of Congress Cataloging-in-Publication Data
Schaef, Anne Wilson.
  When society becomes an addict.
  1. Dependency (Psychology) 2. Social psychology.
I. Title.
BF575.D34S33   1987   302   86–45828
ISBN 0–06–254812–3 (cloth)
ISBN 0–06–254854–9 (paperback)

---

88 89 90 91 92 MPC 10 9 8 7 6 5 4 3

Contents

III. PROCESSES OF THE ADDICTIVE SYSTEM

Acknowledgments

There are many people and processes to acknowledge in the coming into being of this book. This process has been a long labor and a difficult birth. This book is really my second and it is coming out third. In the process of writing this book, I have become a writer, a re-writer, and an editor for which I will be eternally grateful. I want to thank the persons who have nurtured me along this path. Diane Fassel and John Reed have provided encouragement, support, and tough criticism when most needed. The process network and the trainees have given freely of their ideas, their experiences, and themselves. They and the participants at the intensive workshops have freely shared their lives with me for which I am deeply honored. Ugis Pinka, Carolyn Schrodes, and Carol Barrett have helped me become a writer, and Beth and Roddy, my grown children, continue to say, "Go for it, Mom."

Professionally Jan Johnson, Tom Grady, and Clayton Carlson have helped me to know what is possible.

Writing books requires support and I have had it.

I appreciate and am touched by the loving support I have in my life.

WHEN SOCIETY BECOMES AN ADDICT

I. THE ADDICTIVE SYSTEM

Throughout the book, I have changed identifying details and created composites for illustrative purposes.

INTRODUCTION

Our society is deteriorating at an alarming rate. As we watch the news and read the newspapers, we are increasingly made aware of corruption in high places, financial collapse, and a lack of morality in settings ranging from preschools to meat packing plants. We fear that our children will be stolen by child pornography rings, and we hear of our "healers" taking sexual advantage of their clients. Our planet is being destroyed by acid rain and pollution, and nuclear holocaust is a very real possibility. Hunger and wars rage over the planet.

As a society, we are responding not with action but with a widespread malaise. The market for antidepressants has never been better. Apathy and depression have become synonymous with adjustment. Rather than looking for ways to change, to save ourselves, we are becoming more conservative, more complacent, more defensive of the status quo.

Those few individuals who notice and draw attention to these growing problems are met with massive denial. When they run for public office, they are not elected. When they confront us with what they know, they are ignored, dismissed, or discredited.

Other persons attempt to analyze and combat these problems by writing about them. Recent years have seen a proliferation of books expressing their concern from every field of study: *Why Democracies Perish, The Reenchantment of the World, The One Straw Revolution, Turning Point, Entropy, Megatrends,* and *Green Paradise Lost* are just a few.[1]

How-to books on subjects ranging from weight control to psychological self-help are more popular than ever. All try to give us answers, and none really addresses the problem.

I believe that there are two reasons this is true. First, most, if not all, stop at analysis and go no further. The thinking behind them is almost exclusively "left-brain"—rational and logical. To para-phrase Morris Berman in *The Reenchantment of the World,* they come out of a nonparticipatory, scientific approach that is based upon empiricism and logical positivism. This approach is quite limited; it views the world through a very narrow set of lenses.

Second, most, if not all, deal with only one piece of the problem. No one as yet has put the pieces together and treated the problem as a whole. In fact, I suspect that no one has yet perceived the problem as a whole—or, at least, seen it for what it is.

Much of what we know about our society can be compared to what the blind persons knew about the elephant. As that old story teaches us, an elephant is more than just ears, a tail, or a trunk; it is more, even, than just an animal. It is also a process within a context. It is born, it lives, and it dies. This is a process.

The context of our elephant—our society—is the fact that the system in which we live is an addictive system. It has all the characteristics and exhibits all the processes of the individual alco-holic or addict. It functions in precisely the same ways. To say the society is an addictive system is not to condemn the society, just as an intervention with an alcoholic does not condemn the alco-holic. In fact, those of us who work with addicts know that the most caring thing to do is not to embrace the denial and to con-front the disease. This is the only possibility the addict has to recover. Just as with the addict, one has to say that the society *has* a disease. It is not itself the disease. If it admits *having* the disease, it has the option of recovery.

This awareness that society has an addictive disease is what is missing from other explanations and treatments of the problems we are facing today. Most other concerned writers focus only on their specific area of interest or expertise. This is the norm within a fragmented society such as ours. It is also characteristic of the tunnel vision of the alcoholic/addict.

In addition, most people who look at the system are too close to it and too involved in it to see it clearly. They are frequently themselves functioning addicts (in ways I will go on to make clear), come from addictive, dysfunctional families, or they have tried to step outside the system and be "objective," which only serves to keep them uninformed and nonparticipating.

In order to perceive the Addictive System for what it is, one must be *in* it but not *of* it. In other words, one must be recovering from its effects. There are people who fit this criterion. Historically, however, the main curing agent for addictions has been anonymous—Alcoholics Anonymous, Al-Anon, Overeaters Anonymous, Gamblers Anonymous, and so on. As a result, the people who have the most accurate perceptions of our system have often hidden this knowledge in anonymity.

It is impossible to come to a real understanding of anything without actively participating in it. My work in the women's movement and the chemical dependency field has taught me that the most reliable information is that which comes from people with personal experience. Objectivity is a myth. The people who can be trusted the most are those who can honestly say, "I know how you feel because I have been there myself."

When one brings personal participation to the generation of theory, the outcome is synthesis. This book is a synthesis of ideas and experience.

The good news is that, like the individual alcoholic/addict, the Addictive System can recover. Before that can happen, though, we must name and accept the disease. We must admit that the society we care about has a disease and can recover from that disease.

We must also be willing to do the necessary work toward recovery. This is a long process that eventually requires a shift to a new system, one I call the Living Process System.

Before being ready for recovery, the individual alcoholic/addict must often "hit bottom." I believe that our society is rapidly approaching this point, and that it may now be ready for the ideas discussed here.

Part I outlines my personal journey toward the awareness that our system is an addictive system, and that the Addictive System and the White Male System are one and the same. The remainder of Part I then provides a general introduction to addiction. Relationship addiction is used as a model because it is one with which most of us can easily identify. This section also introduces the concept of co-dependence and how it relates to addiction.

Part II names the characteristics of addiction and illustrates how they exist and function within both the individual and the system. Until now, these characteristics have been articulated only in the circles of those who treat addictions. Even there, they have never been gathered together and linked so as to describe an entire system.

To my knowledge, the awareness that larger systems such as schools, churches, businesses, and governments exhibit the same characteristics, processes, problems, and outcomes as the individual alcoholic/addict is new and revolutionary. So, too, is the awareness that these characteristics, processes, problems, and outcomes are prevalent within our system as a whole.

Part III deals with the processes of the addictive system. These processes are insidious and are what hold the system together and keep it functioning. Since the system does not think in terms of processes, partly because processes cannot be measured and controlled, and the system does not conceptualize in terms of processes because this kind of conceptualizing requires participation, it is largely unaware of the stranglehold these processes have on it.

Part IV introduces several new concepts, including paradigm shifts, as well as older concepts like the Alcoholics Anonymous Twelve-Step Program, and suggests some ways they can be used to work toward systemic recovery.

Like my first book, *Women's Reality: An Emerging Female System in a White Male Society,* this is a book of naming and, also, renaming. It explores our system and provides us with a way to understand it. Understanding is the first step toward change.

LOOKING BACK AT *WOMEN'S REALITY*

Because *When Society Becomes an Addict* builds upon some of the ideas put forth in *Women's Reality,* it is useful to begin by briefly returning to those ideas.[2]

Women's Reality identified and described three systems: the White Male System, the Emerging Female System, and the Reactive Female System, as I then called them.

I called the system in which we live the White Male System because the power and influence in it are held by white males, and it is perpetuated by white males—with the help of all of us. As the prevailing system within our culture, it runs our government, our courts, our churches, our schools, our economy, and our society. I want to emphasize here that I am not talking about individuals. I am talking about a system that all of us have learned and in which we all participate. There are as many White-Male-System women as there are men operating in our culture today. I am talking about a system, a worldview.

This system is supported and sustained by four myths. The first myth is that *the White Male System is the only thing that exists.* Hence, the White Male System defines itself as reality, and when someone lives out of another system, that person is said not to understand "reality" or not know "how things are." The beliefs and perceptions of other systems—including the Black System, the Chicano System, the Asian-American System, the Native American System, and both female systems—are unknown to the White Male System and dismissed as irrelevant, inconsequential, or crazy.

The second myth is that *the White Male System is innately superior.* Anyone who does not operate according to this system is by definition innately inferior. This is a confusing myth, because if the White Male System is the only system that exists (reality), what is it superior to? We will see however, that since this system generates its own rules it need not be logically consistent. And often it is not.

The third myth is that *the White Male System knows and understands everything.* This myth means that anything that is not known and understood by the methods and technology of the White Male System theoretically does not exist. This myth defines what knowledge is and what is worth learning. It also defines large areas of knowledge out of existence.

The fourth myth is that *it is possible to be totally logical, rational, and objective.* If one believes it is possible to be logical, rational, and objective, then one ignores the ways one is not and uses only a small part of the brain and senses. The White Male System ignores the existence of and devalues other thinking processes, such as intuition, and multivariate non-linear thinking, which would be considered right-brain or brain stem functions.

All four of these myths can be summarized by another overriding myth: that *it is possible to be God* as defined by the system. If the White Male System is the only system that exists (reality), if it is innately superior to any other system, if it knows and understands everything, and if it values only the logical, rational, and objective, then it can be God as that system defines God. This God is all the "omnis," omnipotent, omniscient, and omnipresent. The major role of this God is that of ultimate controller.

What I have called the White Male System surrounds and envelops us, but it does not feel like "home." In order to survive within it, we must adjust our language, values, and thinking and the way we view the world. We must deny our own reality and surrender our personal power in order to gain a modicum of acceptance.

The female companion system to the White Male System is what I have called the Reactive Female System. This system is a stereotypic, externally defined system that tells women what they should think, feel, and do. It defines women in such a way that they will consciously and unconsciously support the White Male System and its myths. The basic concept of this system is the Original Sin of Being Born Female. In the Reactive Female System, women are taught that they are innately inferior by birth and that there is no absolution except through the intervention of an outside mediator, which is always a man. If women can attach themselves to a male and obtain male validation and approval, then they will be absolved of the Original Sin of Being Born Female. Unfortunately, this never works, but it does not keep us from trying.

Even though there is no "justification by works," we continue to try to make ourselves acceptable by being fair, following the rules, hiding our feelings, and becoming incredibly understanding.

The third system identified in *Women's Reality* is what I called the Emerging Female System. I called it that then because it was a system that I heard from women as they began to trust their own perceptions. The Emerging Female System is variable and changing and would be described in system circles as an open system. It is a system in process, a system *of* process. It is not a new system that we do not know; actually, many people, both women and men, as they move into it describe a feeling of coming "home" to something they have always known and have never been able to articulate.

Women's Reality was a book of naming. Written out of women's awareness and perceptions, it gave us a way to begin communicating about the White Male System, the Reactive Female System, and the Emerging Female System.

That which goes unnamed may exert considerable influence over us, but because we have no words for it we cannot address it directly or deal with it. One example is battering. Only in the last couple of decades have we had a word for battering. It was going on long before then, but it did not functionally exist until it was given a common, agreed-upon name. Nobody talked about it. No one was called a batterer or a victim of battering. No statistics were gathered about it. No safe houses were set up to shelter its victims; no funding was set aside to study or treat it. Once it had a name, though, it became an acknowledged reality in our society. Individuals could say, "I've been battered," or "I've been a batterer." They could talk about their experience and thus validate it.

In her book *The Wizard of Earthsea,* Ursula LeGuin describes how to become a wizard.[3] During the lengthy process of training and education, it is necessary to spend a concentrated block of time with the Master Namer, a teacher who knows the *true* name for everything. The true name is different from the common, public name. When you learn the true name of something, you are able to take back any power it has over you. We need to do that with the system in which we live.

In her book *Silences,* Tillie Olsen points out how our refusal to speak our reality or name our experiences makes us accomplices of a system that oppresses us.[4] Only by naming can we reclaim our reality and our power. We are beginning to do that, too, with the Emerging Female System.

Since writing *Women's Reality,* I have come to see the White Male System, the Reactive Female System, and the Emerging Female System more clearly and to understand more about how they interrelate. I now realize that the White Male System and the Reactive Female System are not two separate systems; instead, they are two aspects of the same system. They cannot exist without each other. They support and perpetuate each other and are part of an inextricable dualism. To move out of the White Male System, one must let go of the Reactive Female System; to let go of the Reactive Female System, one must move out of the White Male System. Neither can be treated as a distinct entity. If there were no White Male System, there would be no need for a Reactive Female System, and if women stopped living in the Reactive Female System the White Male System would collapse. Neither needs to exist without the other, and each must have the other to exist.

In contrast, the Emerging Female System is utterly distinct. It has no relation to the White Male System–Reactive Female System dualism. It exists separately, and functioning within it requires what Marilyn Ferguson, in *The Aquarian Conspiracy,* calls a "paradigm shift."[5] What is fascinating is that despite the need for this paradigm shift, many women and quite a few men already know and understand what I have called the Emerging Female System.

My new awareness has also caused me to revise my thinking about another aspect of *Women's Reality.* In that book, as I was comparing the Emerging Female System with the White Male System, I kept stressing that neither system is right or wrong, good or bad—they are just different. That period was my "fair" phase. I really believed then that neither was right or wrong, and I wanted to be fair.

I no longer believe that. The two systems are not "just different." Instead, what I called the Emerging Female System is life-supporting and life-producing, and what I called the White Male System is nonliving-oriented and entropic.

The White Male System is not only destructive to women; it is destructive to men, animals, plants, and our planet and is threatening to spread its destructiveness into space. The White Male System has a nonliving orientation.

The Emerging Female System is proliving. It embodies the state of being fully alive in the broadest possible sense of the word.

Another issue that has arisen in the years since *Women's Reality* was first published is that of the names I gave the systems. Several people have suggested (some more than "suggested") that I change the names of the systems I described there. Their reasons have varied, and all have had some validity and truth to them: not all males fit into the White Male System; calling the new system the Emerging Female System alienates men; the Emerging Female System is not strictly female; some of the most White-Male-System people are women; the labels *male* and *female* are divisive; and so on. All these points are important.

The use of the labels *male* and *female* has also prompted concern that the Emerging Female System would not be valued as it deserved if it continued to be called "female." In my opinion, this would be the case only for those people who do not value *female* —as a word, as a condition, as a name. It has proved extremely important for women to acknowledge their system as different from the system in which so many men are embedded. It has proved important to call it the Emerging Female System so that women can begin to trust their perceptions, recognize that they are not crazy, and be comfortable with being different. It was important to recognize that all three systems exist and to call them "male" and "female," and now it is time to move on.

Now is the time for renaming. What I called the White Male System–Reactive Female System I am now calling the *Addictive System*. As I have said, it is a system that has a nonliving orientation. What I called the Emerging Female System I am now calling the *Living Process System*. These concepts move beyond the male-female dualism to the exploration of what a nonliving orientation is for all of us, male and female and regardless of race or sexual orientation.

Women's Reality introduced a vocabulary women and men could use to validate our experience and our reality. It named what had previously gone unnamed and made it possible to communicate and to begin reclaiming our power. Now it is time to move on to the next stage of naming.

A PERSONAL ODYSSEY

At about the time that *Women's Reality* was published, my extended family and I became aware that one of our members was an alcoholic. It took us a while to recognize this, because she rarely drank, and everyone knows that alcoholics are always drunk! Also, as the disease progressed our whole household had become confused, chaotic, and crazy. We were so mired in an alcoholic system we could not see it.

We decided to learn about alcoholism. At first we planned to use our knowledge to aid our family member in her recovery. The more we learned, however, the more we came to see that we had contracted the disease ourselves. An alcoholic system—actually, *any* addictive system—is contagious, and those who live within it become infected with the disease sooner or later. The dynamics and patterns are the same for those infected as they are for the alcoholic.

Now we had more to deal with than just our family member's recovery; we had our own to accomplish as well. So we all went through treatment.

Meanwhile I discovered that I had several alcoholics and their families in my private counseling practice, and others started coming to me. I plunged into learning everything I could about alcoholism and other addictions. I read books and pamphlets, went to meetings, attended lectures, and talked to chemical dependency counselors; I compared various approaches, gave lectures of my own, and reflected on my experience.

I began to realize that it is rare for a person to have only one addiction. Instead, the addictive person, or the individual operating within an addictive system, usually has multiple addictions. These work to trap the person in the Addictive System. Even secondary addictions can keep one actively functioning as an addict.

I became aware of how complex each addictive characteristic is. None is as straightforward as it first appears; each has many facets and many levels of truth. Over the next couple of years, as I came to a clearer understanding of these characteristics, I began to say, "That's very similar to the White Male System."

I found myself saying this so frequently that it turned into what I called my "hand-in-glove" theory: the Addictive System and the White Male System fit together like a hand in a glove. I started seeing how the two systems support each other and how the White Male System uses addictions to perpetuate itself. Addictions keep us afraid, out of touch with ourselves, and too busy to challenge the system. No wonder the White Male System accepts them so readily!

Then came the next step in my awareness—one I resisted taking. After some time, as I heard myself repeating, "That's just like the White Male System," I was finally forced to acknowledge that the two are the same. It is not just that they support each other; they *are* each other. There is no difference between them. The White

Male System is the Addictive System; the Addictive System is the White Male System.

Why had I resisted this step? Because as long as I was able to convince myself that the two systems were similar but separate, I did not have to face the enormity of the problem. I could treat alcoholics, put "Band-Aids" on addictions, and go on accepting the White Male System as just different, neither good nor bad. If I acknowledged that the White Male System and the Addictive System were one and the same, I would have to deal with that system as a whole and no longer be "nice" in my complicity with what I had called the White Male System.

That was overwhelming. It meant that the entire system would have to be changed and *must* start recovering. I had seen firsthand how difficult the recovery process was for the alcoholic and the alcoholic family. What would it take for an entire society to recover from being an addict?

I also became aware at about this time that our political culture could be described as an addictive system. The signs were identical to those of alcoholism, only on a far larger scale. This terrified me. I knew how unclear an addict's mind and thinking became; I hated to think that the same addictive thinking might underlie the decisions made for our nation.

I am not referring here just to the alcoholism and drug addiction that continue to be exposed among our national policymakers and lawmakers. I am talking about a whole system that has such elements as confused, alcoholic thinking (AA—Alcoholics Anonymous—calls it "stinkin' thinkin' "), dishonesty, self-centeredness, dependency, and the need for control at its core. Individuals functioning within an addictive system exhibit these characteristics even when they are not personally abusing drink or drugs. These characteristics are dangerous to individuals; imagine how lethal they are when present throughout a system! Just within the fields of chemical dependency, the figures on the extent of alcoholism are overwhelming. I did research on co-dependence as one addictive process among many, and found statistics that support shockingly high levels of co-dependence in our society. For example, Sharon Wegscheider-Cruse, a pioneer in co-dependence research, defines co-dependents as "all persons who (1) are in love or marriage relationships with an alcoholic, (2) have one or more alcoholic parents or grandparents, or (3) grew up in an emotionally repressive family."[6] According to Wegscheider-Cruse, this includes approximately 96 percent of the population. Another expert, Dr. Charles Whitfield, says co-dependence "affects not only individuals, but families, communities, businesses and other institutions, and states and countries."[7] Earnie Larsen, author of *Stage II Recovery,* states that there are between ten and fifteen million alcoholics in this society and that each one directly and adversely affects between twenty and thirty persons.[8] Using his figures, and not accounting for any overlap, we see that the number of co-dependents in the United States exceeds the total population. Both Larsen and Wegscheider-Cruse define co-dependence to the point that it includes the majority of the people in the United States.

As I tried to absorb the impact of these insights, one of my clients presented me with yet another, which helped me pull my thoughts together and added an important dimension.

She had been working on a number of psychological issues and had recently begun confronting her nicotine and relationship addictions. She came to her session one day and announced, "You know, Anne, all these addictions we have been looking at—alcohol, drugs, nicotine, food, relationships, sex, and so on—are all secondary addictions."

"That's very interesting," I replied, somewhat startled. "Tell me what you mean. I'm afraid that AA would not agree with you, as it claims that alcohol is a primary disease that results in death."

"Oh, all addictions will kill you," she said. "Even in an addictive relationship, the stress will kill you. I'm sure that these are all secondary addictions."

She then went on to explain that the primary addictions in the Addictive System are the addictions to powerlessness and nonliving, and that all secondary addictions lead to these two primary addictions.

I asked her to give me an example. She told me that she had grown up in a Southern state and had been raised in a fundamentalist Christian church. Her home and her church were the primary formative institutions in her childhood. In both places, whenever she was "alive"—happy, noisy, full of energy, excited, exuberant, sexual—she was labeled a "bad girl." But whenever she was "dead" or nonliving—quiet, sick, depressed, and showing none of the other signs of "life"—she was labeled a "good girl." She learned that to be alive was bad and to be nonliving was good. To be accepted by her world, she had had to be personally powerless and not alive.

At that point I remembered what another friend, a Ph.D. in literature, had once told me. In doing research for her thesis, she had found that most romantic poetry consists of odes to dead virgins! This fit with what my client was telling me. The ideal woman is the dead virgin. She is neither sexual nor alive.

I found all this very interesting and began putting more pieces together. Those of us who work with addicts know that the very first step toward recovery involves dealing with the choice of dying. Addictions of any type *do* kill, sooner or later. The first choice an addict has to make to start on the path to recovery is the choice not to die.

Those of us who work with addicts also know that choosing not to die is not the same as choosing to live. That is a completely different and separate choice. When we think dualistically, we assume that saying no to one means saying yes to the other, but this is not the case.

At least three combinations of choices are possible. The first is, in a way, the simplest. One can (1) choose not to live and (2) choose to die. The result is usually either suicide or eventual death from addiction.

The second is rare in our system. One can (1) choose not to die and (2) choose to live. The result would be a system change.

The third is the most common. One can (1) choose not to die

and (2) choose not to live. The result is total adjustment to and acceptance of the Addictive System.

We see third-choice people all around us. They are the zombies. They are comfortable in the meaningless jobs of the system. They choose not to die because the system needs them to perpetuate itself and they can therefore fit in.

Choosing to live means that we can no longer support the system as it is. Choosing to live means that we cannot eat much of the food in our supermarkets, breathe the air in many of our cities, allow our groundwater to be polluted by toxic wastes, or sit back and wait for the nuclear holocaust. The Addictive System asks us to accept these things—and more—as inherent to being because they are inherent to the addictive, nonliving system in which we live and hence, "reality."

For most addicts the thought of living—and by this I mean living fully—is far more frightening than the thought of dying or being only partially alive. Since addicts have high control needs, being addicted gives them the illusion of having control (they are in control of being not alive and not dead). Living fully seems the same as having no control, and that feeling is experienced as unbearable.

The Addictive System asks us to become comfortable with actively participating in our own nonaliveness. Addictions take the edge off, block awarenesses that could threaten our seeming equilibrium and allow us to grow, and keep us too busy to challenge the system. They are essential to the system.

There is no question that what I called the White Male System is the Addictive System; the Addictive System is the White Male System. If we love this society in which we live, we must be willing to confront the reality that it has a disease. Like an alcoholic, it is not bad and trying to get good. It is sick and trying to get well.

It is only an archaic understanding of addictions that sees the addict as bad or weak and therefore attempts to ignore the reality and "make up for" the problems. That "niceness" has brought death for many addicts who could have recovered.

It is caring to confront the disease in the individual, and it is caring to confront the disease of the system. By definition, addiction *has control* of the individual. By definition, addiction *has control* of the society.

DEFINING TERMS

Before I go any further, it is necessary to define more fully some of the terms used throughout this book.

ADDICTION

An addiction is any process over which we are powerless. It takes control of us, causing us to do and think things that are inconsistent with our personal values and leading us to become progressively more compulsive and obsessive. A sure sign of an addiction is the sudden need to deceive ourselves and others—to lie, deny, and cover up. An addiction is anything we feel *tempted* to lie about. An addiction is anything we are not *willing* to give up (we may not *have* to give it up *and* we must be *willing to* do so to be free of addiction).

Like any serious disease, an addiction is progressive, and it will lead to death unless we actively recover from it. I shall give some examples of how addiction affects individuals and also what it does at a cultural level.

An addiction keeps us unaware of what is going on inside us. We do not have to deal with our anger, pain, depression, confusion, or even our joy and love, because we do not feel them, or we feel them only vaguely. We stop relying on our knowledge and our senses and start relying on our confused perceptions to tell us what we know and sense. In time, this lack of internal awareness deadens our internal processes, which in turn allows us to remain addicted. At some point we must choose to recover—to arrest the progress of the addiction—or we will die. This dying process does not happen only at a personal level: it is also systemic to our culture.

As we lose contact with ourselves, we also lose contact with other people and the world around us. An addiction dulls and distorts our sensory input. We do not receive information clearly; we do not process it accurately; and we do not feed it back or respond to it with precision. Since we are not in touch with ourselves, we present a distorted self to the world—in AA terms, we "con" people—and eventually lose the ability to become intimate with others, even those we are closest to and love the most.

We are aware that something is very wrong, but the addictive thinking tells us that it could not possibly be our fault. This kind of thinking also tells us that we cannot make things right, that someone else will have to do it for us.

When they cannot (of course), we blame them for what is happening. (On a system level, we believe we are not causing the unrest in the world. If others would only behave, we would not *have to* retaliate.) An addiction absolves us from having to take responsibility for our lives. We assume that someone—or something—outside ourselves will swoop down to make things better or help us to deal with what we are going through. Since addicts tend to be dependent and to feel increasingly powerless and bad about themselves, the notion that they can take responsibility for their lives is inconceivable to them.

The longer we wait to be rescued, the worse our addiction becomes. Regardless of what we are addicted to, it takes more and more to create the desired effect, and no amount is ever enough.

Addictions can be divided into two major categories: substance addictions and process addictions. Both function in essentially the same way and produce essentially the same results. Although I shall describe each separately, it is important to remember that addictions are quite common in our culture and that most addicts have multiple addictions. Although not all addictions are of equal severity, all eventually exhibit similar behavioral dynamics and processes and lead to death.

SUBSTANCE ADDICTIONS

Substance addictions—I also call these "ingestive addictions"—are addictions to substances, usually artificially refined or produced, that are deliberately taken into the body. These substances are almost always mood-altering and lead to increased physical dependence.

Alcohol

Alcohol addiction may be the most common chemical dependency; it is certainly the best documented and understood. Treatment professionals call it a "primary addiction," a disease that will sooner or later lead to death if it is allowed to progress unchecked.

How and when does alcoholism begin? No one knows for certain, although some people in AA maintain that alcoholics are alcoholics long before they take their first drink. What is known is that alcoholics at some point start abusing alcohol—drinking for the specific purpose of altering a mood and/or staying out of touch with their feelings and thoughts. What may at one time have been casual use moves into abuse, and abuse moves into addiction.

Drugs

In our drug-happy society a person can start taking drugs for any number of reasons: to relieve pain or anxiety, to stifle fear, or to put reality in a better light.

Any mood-altering drug has the potential for being addictive. Many people believe that only the illegal ones—heroin, marijuana, cocaine, and street drugs, uppers and downers—are dangerous; in fact, prescription drugs such as Valium, Librium, and Empirin with codeine can be just as addictive. There can come a point at which use moves into abuse.

Any drug taken for the specific purpose of altering a mood and/or avoiding one's inner feelings can become an addictive substance no matter what its original purpose may have been.

Nicotine and Caffeine

Nicotine and caffeine are not as deadly (at least initially) as alcohol and drugs, but they can be just as addictive, both physically and emotionally.

Nicotine and caffeine can be used for essentially the same purpose as any other ingested chemical substance: to "take the edge off," to "push things down," to "give a lift," in other words, to alter moods and mask feelings. Since they kill less quickly and lead to less obvious self-destructive and interpersonally destructive behavior, they have not received as much attention, although public awareness is changing.

Alcohol, drugs, nicotine, and caffeine may be the best-known addictive substances, but they are not the *only* addictive substances. There are plenty of other things we ingest that function much the same as mood-altering chemicals. Sugar can be a "fix"; so can salt. Even food can be a problem; food addictions are gaining more recognition and present more difficulties for recovery.

Food

When use moves into abuse, food becomes an addictive substance and eating becomes compulsive and out of control, a way of avoiding taking responsibility for oneself.

Treating food addictions can be especially difficult, since food is essential to life and the addict cannot withdraw from it completely in order to recover.

To complicate matters further, there are various types of food-related addictions. Overeating may be the most widespread, but two other conditions are becoming more prevalent: anorexia (self-starvation) and bulimia (bingeing and purging). One can be addicted to eating, to *not* eating, or to eating a huge quantity of food and then desperately trying to get rid of it.

People with food-related addictions talk in terms of "burying" what is going on inside of them and "stuffing" their feelings. Food (or the avoidance of food) is perceived as a "cure" for anger, depression, fear, anxiety, and other unpleasant feelings—and for pleasant feelings as well. Many compulsive eaters head for the refrigerator whenever they feel too good or "alive."

PROCESS ADDICTIONS

In a process addiction one becomes hooked on a process—a specific series of actions or interactions. Almost any process can be an addictive agent; those described here are merely examples.

Accumulating Money

In our culture the process of accumulating money often becomes addictive. Like any other addiction it is progressive; it takes more and more to achieve a fix, and eventually no amount is enough.

People caught up in this process use it to avoid dealing with being human and confronting human feelings. They look outside for a solution rather than face the feelings inside. Often they do not care about money in and of itself; what drives them is the series of actions and interactions involved in accumulating it.

Gambling

Much the same can be said for a gambling addiction. The process becomes more important than the winning or the money.

Like all addicts, compulsive gamblers use their addiction to keep them unaware of their internal feelings. Their lives become progressively more unmanageable. Gambling can be just as addictive as alcohol; although it does not destroy the body, as alcohol does, it is equally capable of destroying a life and of wreaking havoc with relationships.

Sex

Sex has been increasingly identified as an addictive process. More and more people seem to be using sex not as a means of relating but as a way of getting a fix.

For many of the couples I work with in therapy, "getting enough sex" translates into avoiding tensions and feelings. They use sex (and each other) to keep from having to deal with themselves. In some cases the partners believe that sex is something they "deserve" and that their partner "owes" them. When a sex addict gets a fix, it serves the same purpose as a drink or a drug, and the personality dynamics that develop are essentially the same.

Work

Much has been written about workaholics, and we are becoming aware that working—which can be one of the important ways we express ourselves—can also become a negative process.

When work becomes an obsession, compulsive behaviors develop that can be harmful and even death-producing. As in accumulating money, gambling, sex, or any other process addiction, the act itself (working) loses its intrinsic meaning. Although the line between simple overwork and an unhealthy addiction to work is tenuous, it is fairly easy to tell when one has crossed it. The workaholic uses work to avoid dealing with inner and interpersonal life.

Religion

Religion can also be a process addiction. I am not talking here about *being* religious or *being* spiritual. Rather, my concern is with "quick-fix" religions, those that avoid thoughtful prayer, meditation, and dialogue and claim to have all the answers.

The religion addict is very different, inside and out, from the person who is involved in spiritual growth. The religion addict loses touch with personal values and develops behaviors that are the same as those of the alcoholic or drug addict—judgmentalism, dishonesty, and control. Use moves into abuse.

Worry

One of my clients introduced me to the idea that worry could be a process addiction. As we worked together, it became evident that she was completely devoted to worrying.

We made up a "worry list," and over time it grew longer and longer. Every angle of every issue provided new and fertile possibilities. She worried when she felt bad and when she felt good (the good feelings might go away!). She worried about not having enough money (she had plenty) and felt guilty about the money she had (other people were starving!).

One of her biggest worries was that no one would ever love her and she would always be alone. Yet whenever someone tried to get close to her, she became fearful of too much intimacy (she would be swallowed up!). Then she started worrying about whether she was loving the other person "right" and being loved "right" in return. If she made herself vulnerable, the love might go away—or maybe it wouldn't, and then what? Would she be able to handle it?

When she didn't have anything specific to worry about, she felt lost and started looking for a "worry fix." When I asked her what would happen if she stopped worrying, she voiced concern over the possible loss of an "old friend." We both became aware that worry had become an addictive process for her, taking on a life of its own and exhibiting all the signs of an addiction. The content —the reason behind a particular bout of worrying—was far less important than the act of worrying itself.

It should be obvious by now that almost anything, substance or process, *can* become addictive. Television or running also can be addictions. On the other hand, it is equally true that there is nothing that *must* become addictive; it may even be that the whole system that develops in conjunction with a specific addiction is more important than the specific addiction itself.

Because we live in an addictive society, temptation is all around us. The society in which we live needs addictions in order to perpetuate itself. We do have other choices, however (and I hope this book will make them more obvious), but first we must understand our present situation.

SYSTEM

A system is a series of contents and processes that is larger than the sum of its parts. It has a life of its own, distinct from the lives of the individuals within it, and it calls forth certain characteristic behaviors and processes in those individuals.

ADDICTIVE SYSTEM

An addictive system is a system that calls forth addictive behaviors. The individual begins to operate out of an addictive process.

An addictive system is a *closed* system in that it presents few choices to individuals in terms of roles they may take and directions they may pursue.

RELATIONSHIP ADDICTION AS A MODEL FOR THE ADDICTIVE SYSTEM

As I began using these concepts with my clients, it became clear that I needed a model for the Addictive System, one that would include all or most of its characteristics and serve as a reference point.

Many people are understandably sensitive to being compared to alcoholics and drug addicts, even though they share many of the same characteristics, processes, problems, and outcomes simply because they live in the Addictive System. Since this had the potential to interfere with understanding, it was necessary to come up with another way to approach these issues.

Meanwhile I began looking more closely at addictive relationships. I had been in some myself and knew very few people who had not. The more I learned about addictive relationships, the more I realized that they are the norm for our society. Each of us, at some point or another, has some sort of relationship with another human being, and frequently our relationships are addictive.

Here, then, was my model. Relationship addiction was something with which I was intimately involved; I had experienced it, examined my own relationships for symptoms, and worked on the recovery process. I had also treated several relationship-addicted clients.

As I had hoped it would, this model also proved helpful in my practice. When my clients began perceiving certain qualities of their relationships as addictive, this awareness led them to a better understanding of addictions. It also led them to the awareness that the characteristics and dynamics of any addiction are similar to those of any other addiction.

An addictive relationship is the basic relationship within our culture. It is a "cling-clung" relationship. Both persons involved are convinced that they cannot exist without it. They see themselves as two half-persons who must stick together to make a whole. They arrive at decisions in tandem. They practically synchronize their breathing.

We are taught from an early age to call the addictive relationship by another name: true love. True love is when two people are incapable of functioning or even surviving without each other. We are also taught from an early age that the way to attain "security" (a static, nonprocess concept) is by establishing such a mutual dependency. We are accustomed to thinking of women as being dependent, and in fact women are conditioned to seek and move into dependent relationships. Unfortunately, addictive relationships never involve just one dependent person. They require at least two people and cannot continue unless both parties are willing to enter into and live within an addictive system.

Addictive relationships are very powerful and seductive and hard to resist. Though some people actively choose and move into them, others seem to slide into them unaware. In *Women's Reality,* I discussed something I called the American Fairy Tale: the Perfect Marriage. As I noted there, this marriage wears two faces, the public and the private.

In the public Perfect Marriage, the woman is the child and the man is the adult. In this marriage (or relationship—"marriage" is a convenient label, not a requirement), the man (or the person taking the traditional male role in same-sex relationships) makes the decisions, deals with the outside world, earns the money, and determines how it will be spent. The woman (or the person taking the traditional female role) is dependent on the man to cope with the world, provide the livelihood, and keep the car running (and perhaps even drive it, since the woman may not know how to drive). The woman cannot exist without the man. He is essential to her very survival.

In the private Perfect Marriage, the roles are reversed. The man is the child and the woman is the adult. She prepares and serves his food, sees that he is clothed (and often does his shopping for him), meets his sexual needs, takes care of his social needs, and even protects him from his own children when he needs quiet. He is physically and emotionally dependent on her.

Neither partner is liable to walk out on the other because each fully believes that he or she could not live without the other. They have achieved the security and constancy they have been taught to think they must achieve. Each encourages the other's dependency out of fear of being left behind and alone. Each is reluctant to act independently out of fear of threatening the stability of the relationship.

The relationship functions as an addiction, and it is expected to meet all the needs of both individuals involved. It is used as a fix to keep each person out of touch with what is actually going on inside.

We can see the addictive process in action when an addictive relationship breaks up and each person scrambles to get another fix—a new relationship—as soon as possible. They believe that this will make it possible to avoid going through the painful and natural grieving process that accompanies the ending of an important relationship. The fix keeps them unaware of what is going on inside. The trouble is that finding something outside does not make things all right again. The pain and grieving go on anyway, and new relationships have little chance of succeeding.

An addictive relationship is, by definition, a *permanent* parent-child/child-parent relationship. It cannot survive if either person becomes a whole person or a full adult and takes responsibility for her- or himself. It is jeopardized if either person begins to grow or change.

According to AA, alcoholics cannot stay static. They must either get better or get worse. Both addiction and recovery are processes. The goal of the addictive relationship, however, is security and therefore stasis. The relationship addict is invested in the idea of security and holds onto the illusion of security even when it becomes obvious that the relationship is deteriorating. A relationship is *never* static; it is either getting better or getting worse. Its very nature is dynamic. It is a process, not a product. Therefore it is difficult if not impossible to keep it static.

Once we accept that addictive relationships are the norm for our society, we begin to see how our society works to reinforce and encourage them. Our popular music is an excellent example of this norm. I think that country and western music is the worst, but rock and pop show the same traits. The relationships described in these songs are almost invariably addictive. The two most common themes are instant love (or instant intimacy) and suffering. The message is that true love happens on first contact ("at first sight"—like being zapped) and that one must suffer to be in love. Look at the titles: "Some Enchanted Evening," "One Has My Name, the Other Has My Heart," "I Can't Live Without You," "I Am Addicted to You."

It is significant that many of these songs become part of our lives during adolescence, an age when we are first testing our identity and starting to explore relationships with others. We know that music affects a different part of the brain than the spoken or written word. What kind of brainwashing about relationships is occurring when we are exposed to these songs again and again? All the characteristics of addictive relationships are drummed into our heads until we hear nothing else: "I can't survive without you," "love is suffering," "I am nothing without you." These themes condition us to accept addictive love as true love, as the only way to love and be loved. To love is to become addicted, we are taught to believe.

No wonder we fail to find love that is healthy and dynamic and alive; no wonder we end up singing the sad songs.

THE ADDICTIVE SYSTEM AND CO-DEPENDENCE

No discussion of an addictive system is complete without a close look at co-dependence.[9]

Sharon Wegscheider-Cruse has, I think, done more work on co-dependence than anyone in the country. In an unpublished work, she defines co-dependence as "an addiction to another person or persons and their problems, or to a relationship and its problems."[10] She notes that co-dependence is now being recognized by some insurance companies as a primary disease; that has an onset, a definable course, and a predictable outcome. In other words, co-dependence is not a symptom of something else.

A co-dependent is a person who is currently involved in a love or marriage relationship with an addict, had at least one alcoholic parent or grandparent, and/or grew up in an emotionally repressive family. According to Wegscheider-Cruse, co-dependents make up about 96 percent of the population.

In the last several years, the treatment of addictions has moved toward recognizing that it is not enough to treat the individual who is abusing alcohol, drugs, or whatever it is. Instead, we must treat the individual's whole family system, which is an addictive system. As a result more emphasis is being placed on treating the co-dependent.

Co-dependence is a very interesting disease in itself. Not only is it supported and encouraged by our culture; it is seen as the positive way to function within it. The Addictive System views co-dependence as normal, proof that one has embraced the system and everything it implies.

THE CHARACTERISTICS OF CO-DEPENDENCE

The co-dependent is invariably a Good Person. Co-dependents are devoted to taking care of others within the family system, and often beyond; many become professional caregivers (nurses, doctors, counselors). According to Wegscheider-Cruse, 83 percent of all nurses are firstborn children of alcoholics and, therefore, co-dependents by definition.[11] (Wegscheider-Cruse also points out that many treatment centers exhibit hostility toward co-dependents and reluctance to treat them; the reason often is that the people who run the centers are themselves untreated co-dependents.)

Co-dependents frequently have feelings of low self-worth and find meaning in making themselves indispensable to others. They are willing to do whatever it takes to be liked. As a result their caretaking often progresses to the point of workaholism. They throw themselves into their work (especially if they are in the caregiving professions) and often overwork.

Co-dependents are sufferers—Good Christian Martyrs. Their goodness is directly related to their suffering and the rewards they expect (and receive) because they are willing to sacrifice so much. They are always putting others first, taking the smallest piece of pie, wearing old clothes.

Co-dependents are servers. They are the volunteers, the people who hold the society together, who set aside their own physical, emotional, and spiritual needs for the sake of others. They end up overburdened and exhausted, and we see them as heroes.

Co-dependents are selfless to the point of hurting themselves. They work and care for others to such an extreme that they develop all kinds of physical and emotional problems. Then—and only then—do they allow *themselves* to be cared for and nurtured. Co-dependents tend to have ulcers, high blood pressure, colitis, back pain, and rheumatoid arthritis; they are at high risk for cancer. Co-dependents who are children tend to develop allergies, skin problems, asthma, bed-wetting, and learning disabilities and are frequently accident-prone or suicidal.

What else do co-dependents get in return for their efforts? The answer reveals another fascinating side to the story: The people they care for become dependent on them!

Co-dependents not only have relationships with addicts; they exhibit many of the same characteristics as addicts. They may not use alcohol or drugs, but they do use other substances compulsively and addictively. Co-dependents are frequently anorexic or bulimic or have other eating disorders. They often smoke heavily, or drink gallons of coffee. Co-dependence is simply another side of the same old coin.

I have worked with many active and recovering co-dependents, and like most people in this field I believe that they can be harder to treat than alcoholics. Recovering addicts who are also recovering co-dependents claim that the latter disease is more difficult to deal with. It is very subtle and insidious, and it is perceived very differently by our culture. Alcoholism and other addictions are viewed as negative and bad, but co-dependence is actually fostered. The co-dependent receives little encouragement to get well because the disease supports the culture and is supported by it.

The Addictive System could not survive without its co-dependents. They are the people who keep it going; they are its advocates and its protectors.

Another characteristic common to co-dependents is gullibility. Co-dependents believe that people are telling them the truth even when they are obviously lying. They want to be good; they want to be liked; they want to be included; and these motives are so powerful that they take precedence over judgment. They cannot see when they are being tricked, lied to, or deceived, because they do not choose to see.

As a result co-dependents do not respect others. Since many of us are confused as to what respect really is, I shall illustrate this with an example from my own life.

I have a friend who used to be a compulsive liar. For years I demanded that she stop lying to me (control!). I believed that I was the only person she lied to (self-centeredness!). Then one day I witnessed her lying to another person for whom she cared a great deal.

I suddenly realized that she not only lied to cover up, she also lied for no reason, and her lying had nothing to do with me. Since I had little training in dealing with lying, I told her that I wanted to pull back from our friendship for a while. When my skills improved (when my recovery from my own co-dependence was further along), and/or when she became more honest, we could start spending time together again.

As soon as I said this, she burst into tears and said that this was the first time anyone had understood her. Up until that moment I had seen her as I wanted her to be and refused to see her as she was. I had not respected her or her reality; instead, I had insisted that she accept mine. I had been controlling and disrespectful toward her.

The Addictive System invites us to be co-dependents, to refuse to see people and things as they are. In doing so we are fundamentally disrespectful of them. It is only when people are seen as they are that they can accept and honor and take responsibility for themselves. It is only when they own who they are that they have the option to become something else.

Co-dependents share numerous other characteristics and behaviors with the alcoholic or addict. The difference is that in the co-dependent these are considered acceptable. Co-dependents simultaneously exhibit some of the most valued and some of the most despised characteristics in our culture. The latter are usually abhorred in women and ignored in men. The dishonesty of the co-dependent is perceived as niceness, righteousness, correctness, and the ability to be understanding; the selflessness of the co-dependent is often dishonesty in disguise. Rather than coming right out and saying what they want, co-dependents use devious and indirect means. They avoid facing an issue if it is at all possible. They talk around and *about* people, not *to* them. They use rumor, innuendo, and gossip to manipulate others and cause confusion. In our society, these behaviors are considered normal and being nice.

CO-DEPENDENCE AS PART OF THE OVERALL SYSTEM

What is now defined as the disease of co-dependence is the result of years of training. The Good Christian Martyr is the product of careful grooming. Co-dependence training is simply another form of basic training for the Addictive System. They cannot exist without each other. When people refuse to be co-dependents, addictions do not get the support they need to continue. When addicts are recovering, they can no longer tolerate living with or being around co-dependents. When both make a system shift as part of their recovery, the Addictive System begins to collapse.

I have said the White Male System and the Addictive System are one and the same. It follows, then, that if the Reactive Female System supports the White Male System and co-dependence supports the Addictive System, there must be some relationship between the Reactive Female System and co-dependence. In fact, there is: they, too, are the same.

What this means is that everything I described in *Women's Reality* as belonging to the White Male System and the Reactive Female System also holds true for the Addictive System and co-dependence. In addition, everything I am saying here about the Addictive System and co-dependence fits with the White Male System and the Reactive Female System.

What this means is that we can no longer label one, or treat one, or see one without acknowledging the presence of all the others. It is not enough to treat alcoholism or drug dependency or even co-dependence. If we are to change our orientation from nonliving to living, we must treat the system as a whole.

II. THE ADDICTIVE SYSTEM AS A HOLOGRAM

INTRODUCTION

The White Male System is the Addictive System; the Addictive System is the White Male System. They are one and the same, signifying that the system in which we live has set our society on the path toward nonliving.

It is important and useful to approach the concept of the Addictive System as a hologram. The new holographic paradigm is an approach to science and understanding the world that is nonlinear; it is coming out of the new work in physics and brain physiology.[1] The essential feature of a hologram is that each piece of the hologram contains the entire structure of the entire hologram; each piece is not just a part of the whole, it has the entire pattern and way of functioning of the whole embedded in it. This is a useful way to look at the Addictive System. The system is like the individual, and the individual is like the system. In other words, the Addictive System has all the characteristics of the individual alcoholic/addict. And because we live in this system, every one of us, unless recovering by means of a system shift, exhibits many of these same characteristics.

This part of the book names and describes the characteristics of an addict and illustrates how they function within both the individual and the system as a whole.

SELF-CENTEREDNESS

Addicts are notoriously self-centered. They may claim to care about the people around them, but their fix begins to overshadow everything else. The alcoholic thinks only of the next drink, the relationship addict of the next affair, the workaholic of the next item on the agenda. The Addictive System considers self-centeredness a virtue.

Self-centeredness has many facets, the most obvious of which is a total lack of consideration for others. Not too long ago I witnessed a shocking example. I was taking a nap beside a hot mineral pool when I was awakened by someone making a great deal of noise. A mother had brought her young son to the pool, and she was banging a lounge chair around. She clearly did not care that she was causing a disturbance.

She also did not care about her son's needs. I overheard her telling someone else what had brought the two of them to the pool. Her son had pulled a muscle, and she had kept him out of school for the day to give him a chance to soak in the hot water. When they arrived, she learned that children were not allowed in the pool. By now, however, *she* wanted to stay.

There was only one chair that was not in use; *she* took it and told her son to sit on the concrete until another became available. He obeyed and happily began listening to music on his earphones. The mother asked if she could hear "just a little"; he handed the radio to her, and she kept it for half an hour.

He then asked if he could have the soft drink that she had packed for him. She took it out of a bag and gave it to him. He opened it, took a drink, carefully set it on his chair (he had managed to find one), and wandered off.

In his absence the mother picked up the drink and finished it. When the child came back and found it empty, an amazing conversation ensued.

"It's all gone!" the boy said.

"I only had a little sip," his mother answered.

"But it's all gone!"

"Well, maybe I had a big sip, but I didn't drink it all."

"You did drink it all!"

"Stop whining. I'll get you another one later."

"But I'm thirsty now!"

"I said later!" his mother shouted.

The child's needs were every bit as pressing as his mother's (actually, I thought, *more* pressing), but that did not concern her at all.

Unfortunately, self-centeredness is contagious. When we are around people who care little about us, it becomes important to protect our turf, hoard our belongings, and think only of ourselves, because no one else will. I could imagine the boy growing up to believe that he had to be selfish or he would never have anything.

I witnessed a rather amusing example of self-centeredness recently on a whale watch. One of the participants became progressively depressed and withdrawn. When I inquired what was wrong, she stated that she had spent all this money and come all this way and the whales did not even notice she was there! This is self-centeredness!

Another aspect of self-centeredness puts the self at the center of the universe. Everything that happens is perceived as being either for or against the self.

Some years ago when I was married, I often needed some time alone (I still do, we all do!). Whenever I expressed this need to my husband, he would say, "Why do you want to go away from me?" I would try to explain that I was *not* "going away from him"; I was going *to* myself, and it had nothing to do with him. He was assuming that everything I did was either for or against him.

We all have plenty of opportunities to be self-centered. In our culture, self-centeredness is accepted and even encouraged, and for me it often becomes a matter of fighting a learned behavior. Whenever I speak in front of an audience, for example, there is usually at least one person who gets up and leaves the room for some reason. It would be easy to assume that the person's leaving had something to do with me. Most likely, however, it does not. (I know, because I have often walked out on a speaker for reasons entirely my own.)

This kind of self-centeredness operates on a national level and is prevalent among the people in our government. Everything that happens in the world is perceived as being either for or against the United States. Actions in the Middle East, in Central America, in

Africa are all directed at us or in opposition to us, or so our leaders seem to believe. Having bought into the Addictive System, they cannot help but think this way.

Still another aspect of self-centeredness has to do with what clinical professionals call ego boundaries. Self-centered people do not know where they begin and end and anyone else begins and ends. Self-centered people cannot respect others, because they literally are unaware of them as separate entities. (We can clearly see this on an international level.)

Because there are no clear-cut boundaries, two things happen: the self spreads out, and the world rushes in. Everything becomes ME (in *Women's Reality* I called this the pseudopodic ego), and everything starts coming at ME and is perceived as either for or against ME.

The first is overwhelming; the second is terrifying and leads to the feeling of needing to control. Later I will discuss the illusion of control, but for now it should be evident why self-centered people tend to be very controlling. They feel that they *must* be in order to protect themselves from a universe that they perceive may overpower them.

As I began learning about self-centeredness as described by AA and in the literature about other types of addictions, I saw almost immediately that everything about it applies to the Addictive System.

In the Addictive System *the self is central.* Everyone and everything else must go through, be related to, and be defined by the self as perceived by the self. Addictive System persons find it difficult or even impossible to be objective (though they are always correcting for subjectivity) or to see another's perspective. They do not know how; they cannot learn because the self is always in the way and they cannot get past it.

In the Living Process System *relationships are central.* Living Process System persons are in a constant state of transcending the self. Because relationships are philosophically conceived of as peer until proven otherwise, each new encounter holds the promise of equality. People who perceive each other as equals form the habit of seeing self and others and seeing and respecting each other's points of view.

Another aspect of self-centeredness is arrogance. The Addictive System is quite arrogant. Like the White Male System, it really believes that it is possible to be God as defined by that system. In holding this belief, it also assumes that it has the right to define everything, which is the epitome of self-centeredness. Addicts are arrogant. The Addictive System is arrogant. We even see this arrogance on a national level.

THE ILLUSION OF CONTROL

One of the major pitfalls of any addiction is the illusion of control.

In an addictive system everyone tries to control everyone else. The family tries to control the addict, the addict tries to control the family, the spouse tries to control against being controlled; everyone is involved in some sort of manipulative behavior. The worse the addiction becomes, the more desperate the need for control. The belief that anyone can get a handle on it is an illusion.

Addictive relationships are founded on the illusion of control. Many people are convinced that they are not loved unless the loved one is trying to control them. They define love as either controlling or being controlled. This attitude is particularly obvious in adolescent girls, some of whom literally do not know what to do unless their boyfriends tell them.

One of my teenage friends described what happened the first time he took a certain young woman out on a date. They were riding in his car when he asked her what she wanted to do for the evening.

"Whatever you want," she said.

"Well," the young man answered, "do you want to go to a party, go to a movie, rent a movie and go home and watch it, or what?"

"Whatever you want," she repeated.

He stopped the car in the middle of the street and said, "If you are going to go out with me, you have to have an opinion."

He was not interested in starting a controlling-controlled relationship. This is rare in our culture. Most people believe that relationships *should* revolve around control.

We often confuse control with responsibility. When we talk about "taking responsibility" within a relationship, we often mean taking control over all of the decisions made about it (such as what to do for the evening).

In the Living Process System responsibility is *the ability to respond.* In the Addictive System responsibility involves *accountability and blame.* The common belief is that responsible people are "in charge" and should be able to control everything. It therefore follows that they should be held accountable and blamed if something does not go as planned. If that is how we perceive responsibility, no wonder it seems like such a burden!

We also confuse control with power. In *Women's Reality,* I said that the White Male System concept of power was that of power *over,* while the Emerging Female System concept of power was that of *personal* power and had nothing to do with power over anything. To borrow from an old saying, personal power ends where the other person's nose begins. But even our (Addictive System) dictionaries define power as "ascendancy *over* others." We learn to equate power with authority, domination, and sovereignty; in fact, these are all synonyms for it. The Living Process System is beginning to reclaim the word.

The illusion of control is prevalent within any addictive system. We are all subject to it, even when we are sure we have gone far beyond it in our own personal development. I was made painfully aware of this illusion when a friend came to visit and stayed with me for two weeks. At the time she was very much functioning in addictive patterns, and although I thought I was long out of mine and "safe," I slipped right back into them.

I began to feel as though my house were falling apart around me. I described this to another friend, "It's as if I'm sitting in the middle of a hot stove, surrounded by pots with their lids popping off, and I'm trying to keep the lids on!"

The illusion of control is only an illusion, because none of us can really control anything. We think we can, we think we should be able to, we think we ought to try, and we cannot.

In an addictive system the illusion of control starts with an attempt to control the self with a substance or a process. Drinking, taking drugs, worrying, working late, and having affairs are perceived as ways to avoid dealing with what one is thinking, feeling, and doing. They quickly expand into attempts to control what others are thinking, feeling, and doing.

For instance, a lot of people firmly believe that they can *make* someone love them. They forget that love is a gift that must be freely given. Instead, they get involved in saying the "right" things, wearing the "right" clothes, and behaving in the "right" ways. They think that they have the power to change someone else's mind and arouse the desired feelings in that person.

This belief is so common within our culture that many people would rather feed their illusion of control than risk getting what they want. If they find that they are more successful at making people dislike or even hate them, they opt for that. My definition of true neurotics is those who would rather feed their illusion of control than take the risk of getting what they want.

It is staggering to realize how heavily we are invested in something that simply does not exist. I suppose that is why the first step of the AA Twelve-Step Program involves admitting that one is powerless over the addiction, and that one's life is unmanageable in relation to it. Coming to grips with the illusion of control is essential to recovery.

The illusion of control is closely linked to three other characteristics of an addictive system: crisis orientation, depression, and stress.

CRISIS ORIENTATION

Addicts and their families live from crisis to crisis. Every event or issue is perceived as a major turning point, and one barely ends when the next one begins.

I have believed for some time that crises serve the purpose of giving addicts and their families the illusion of being alive. When they have a crisis, they are at least feeling something.

Actually, crisis orientation is also a very subtle form of control. Creating a crisis feeds our illusion of control because the crisis is something *we* have created. Even when the situation gets out of control, it is satisfying to us because it is *our* situation and *we* made it. A skilled crisis-causer can weave a crisis out of the most mundane event. Getting the kids off to school, making a decision on the job, planning what to have for dinner, telephoning a friend—everything is done in a state of panic.

A colleague of mine is becoming aware of how frequently she turns ordinary living into a crisis. As she struggles to confront her own illusion of control, she is finding that she has fewer crises to contend with. The more quickly one relinquishes the illusion of control, the less crisis-oriented one's life becomes.

We see this crisis orientation on a system level, also. There is no doubt that a crisis is good for the economy and keeps the public believing that our government is "doing something." Sometimes we need to create a crisis to give ourselves a role and feel needed.

DEPRESSION

Once as I flew to a speaking engagement I happened to be seated next to a director of a mental health center. We began talking about our work, and he mentioned that whenever anyone came to his clinic suffering from depression, he automatically checked for alcoholism in the individual or in the family.

Impressed (and somewhat shocked), I asked him to explain. He replied that he had found that when the presenting problem was depression, the real diagnosis was frequently alcoholism or alcohol-related.

I filed this idea away in my mental computer, thinking that I would refer to it the next time I worked with a depressed client. An opportunity came very soon.

One of my clients was the wife of a recovering alcoholic. She was working on recovering from her co-dependence. As we explored her depression, I began to see that it was directly related to her illusion of control.

Her life was a mess. She could not control the behavior of her husband, who was in early recovery and having a hard time of it. She could not control the behavior of the other family members, who were struggling with life in an alcoholic system. But she *thought* she should be able to control them all. Her depression had grown out of her inability to do something she firmly believed was possible.

Once we began confronting the illusion of control, my client was able to recover from her depression quite quickly. Her recovery program had taught her the serenity prayer: "Lord, grant me the serenity to accept the things I cannot change/The courage to change the things I can/and the wisdom to know the difference." This prayer helped her to put her control issues into perspective.

The illusion of control is a setup for depression. When we believe that we can and should be able to control our world and it turns out that we cannot (which is always the case), we experience failure, and this is depressing. We then try even harder to gain control and fail even more miserably.

Anyone trying to recover from an addiction or life within an addictive system must come to terms with control issues; it is an essential part of the recovery process.

STRESS

There is a great deal of interest these days in stress, its causes, and its effects—which include death. I have observed in myself and my clients that almost all stress is a by-product of the illusion of control.

Another time I was flying to a speaking engagement, the man next to me initiated a conversation. I told him the purpose of my trip and explained that I would be speaking at a medical school. As it turned out, it was where he worked, teaching physiology and doing workshops on stress.

"It sounds as if we're working on some of the same things," I said. "We live in an unnecessarily stressful society, and tomorrow I'll be presenting the option of a far less stressful—maybe even stress-free—system."

He puffed up and said, "That's impossible!"

"Wouldn't you like a system that was free of stress and easier to live in?" I asked.

"No," he said. "Some stress is necessary to any system; sometimes it's even good for it."

I was astonished. "How could you possibly believe that?"

"Stress kills off the weaklings and ensures survival of the fittest," he said.

For me this conversation was now at an end. I had nothing further to say, other than "Really? Do you know statistically which one of us will die first?"

He did not attend my lecture the next day. His conviction that his system was the center of the universe and the *only* system that represented reality is a product of distorted thinking. He even had to distort the facts to maintain his stress-is-necessary illusion. Clearly, he would stick by his story to the end, even if it killed him (which it probably would). A society that operates out of an illusion of control certainly would accept stress as normal.

The illusion of control is directly related to the second, third, and fifth myths of the White Male System.

Myth #2 holds that the White Male System is innately superior. Believing this means, by extension, that everything else is inferior and should be subjugated to that system and *controlled* by it—for its own good.

Myth #3 says that the White Male System knows and understands everything. Anything it does not know and understand cannot, by definition, exist. New or different information cannot be tolerated, since it threatens the myth and the system as a whole. Such information must be concealed or manipulated—*controlled.*

The fifth myth maintains that it is possible to be God as defined by that system. The outstanding characteristic of that particular

God is the ability to *control* everything. He is white, male, and in charge.

In his book *The Courage to Love*, William Sloane Coffin argues against this image of God:

> Consider, for instance, some of the phrases commonly heard in the abortion debate. Take, for example, "sanctity of life." This phrase can be invoked in favor of fetal rights as well as in favor of the human species' right to survival, threatened as it is with overpopulation. Or take the phrase, "God forbids the taking of innocent life." Patently true and another reason for abolishing warfare in the nuclear age, but that still leaves us human beings to define "innocent" and "life." Or, "We cannot play God." Agreed again. But *God* does not play God, as that phrase is generally understood. God does not interfere directly in our affairs as the primary causative agent of our births and deaths. God does not marry us and take us to bed, any more than God goes around firing every murderer's pistol, sitting behind every steering wheel, smoking every cigarette. Of course we cannot play God, but neither can we pretend we are without responsibility, mere passive victims of whatever befalls us. After all, we are "a royal priesthood, a holy nation, God's own people."[2]

The God of the Addictive System, who is the God that religion teaches and who in truth has little in common with the God of the Old and New Testaments, is God the Controller. It follows, then, that if it is possible to be God as defined by that system, one must try to control everything, and we do!

Consider our political leaders. We have a president and a cabinet who believe firmly that they can control everything. Reagan has not only convinced himself that he can control what happens on this planet; he also thinks that he can control outer space!

Because our system envisions God as God the Controller, and because we believe that it is possible to be God, we pattern our lives around the illusion of control. Everyone tries to control everyone else. Our government sees its purpose as regulation and control. Our relationships fall into the controlling-controlled pattern. One of our greatest fears is that of "losing control" of ourselves, our families, our surroundings.

Even our parenting practices aim at controlling, which makes me wonder whether some of the "facts" of child rearing are true in general or only true in an addictive system. For example: Is adolescent rebellion really a "normal" developmental stage? Would teenagers need to rebel to establish their identities if we stopped trying to control them? What would happen if we took a noncontrolling approach to parenting?

Trying to be God has an additional effect: it overstresses the human organism and eventually leads to death. As we try to control those things that are not in our power to control, our bodies become so strained and tense that we literally drop dead. I firmly believe that our lives could be relatively stress-free if we relinquished our illusion of control.

One more aspect of the illusion of control remains to be discussed: its bearing on the medical profession and the healing arts.

THE MEDICAL MODEL

It is no secret that most physicians see themselves as God as defined by that system. They are convinced that they hold the power over life and death. Only recently have people begun to recognize that individuals are actively involved in their own healing process and, in fact, *must* be if healing is to occur.

In my own field—mental health—the focus is usually on getting clients "under control," stopping or controlling their processes. If this process takes the client somewhere else, the therapist actively tries to put the client back on track. If the therapy itself proves insufficient, drugs or other restraints are used.

The therapist's need to control is most evident in dealing with psychotics. I know from personal experience how exhausting psychotics can be; they can also be frightening and very controlling themselves. And I also know that a psychosis can be a productive and meaningful part of a client's process.

I believe that most therapists are afraid of a client's deep process work (not to mention their own!). Very few of the professionals I have observed are capable of dealing with their own emotional responses to disturbed clients, and fewer still are willing to explore their own need for control. Furthermore, therapists in general have little knowledge of or training in the disease process, whether physical or psychological. We are just beginning to explore what it means to *work with* a disease process and not try to control it.

For the past fifteen years I have been developing an approach that I call living process therapy. This therapy bypasses the cognitive and works with other parts of the brain and the being, and then brings everything back to the cognitive for closure. I believe that this process is where healing (not mere adjustment) occurs.

In developing living process therapy, I have become increasingly aware of how dependent Addictive System therapies are on the illusion of control. This dependence is especially evident in Freudian psychoanalysis. What could be more control-oriented than a situation in which the client is forced to lie down, face the other direction, follow the rules, come five times a week, speak when spoken to, and take vacations only when the therapist does?

Even goal setting is a controlling device, regardless of whether the goals are determined by the therapist or by the therapist and the client jointly.

It is somewhat harder to see how the more contemporary therapies (such as Gestalt, primal, conjoint family) fit this model, but they do. Like traditional therapies they have originated within an addictive, controlling system; like traditional therapies they are predicated upon the illusion that the client can be controlled. For example, in some contemporary therapies there have been years of discussion about the "taboo of touch" that exists in the more traditional therapies, and there is a general consensus that touch is necessary and good. However, I have seen several well-known therapists on film and in person use touch to control and shut off a person's process when the therapist was losing control and/or did not know what to do with the client's process. I do not think the issue is whether touching is good or bad. The issue is whether touching or nontouching are used for control and whether control is seen as good and necessary.

Unfortunately, none of these therapies, traditional or contemporary, are doing what they are supposed to do. They are not healing people. Instead, they are fostering co-dependence and preparing people to fit into an addictive society. They are not alleviating the problem; they are perpetuating it.

Our Addictive System prizes control. At the Epcot Center in Orlando, Florida, I went to see the energy exhibit. The illusion of control permeated everything in it. Energy, I heard, was the key to "harnessing the power of the universe." What an idea!

Recovering addicts know that they must relinquish their illusion of control in order to recover. If we are to recover, we must effect a system shift. We must move away from churches that attempt to control our spirituality, schools that attempt to control our beliefs and behavior, and relationships that are defined in terms of who is in control. We must admit that our society is based on the illusion of control and recognize that the system in which we live is an Addictive System.

DISHONESTY

Practicing drunks are consummate liars. They lie about how much, when, where, with whom, and whether. Frequent and habitual lying is one of the more evident signs of alcohol or drug abuse.

Like the drunk, the Addictive System is fundamentally dishonest; it is just more subtle about it.

In working through my ideas on the Addictive System, I have had to familiarize myself with the subtleties of lying. This has not been easy for me. Throughout my childhood I heard how important it was to tell the truth. I found out that no matter what I had done I would always get in less trouble if I told the truth than if

I was caught in a lie, so I grew up with little training in detecting and dealing with lying.

I have had some experience with it since. I worked for a while at what was called the criminally insane ward at Bellevue Hospital in New York City. Because I expected people there to lie, it was fairly easy to catch them doing it. I have also known and lived with some of the most accomplished liars around, and my lie-detecting skills have greatly improved!

THE THREE LEVELS OF LYING

I have learned that the first level of lying is lying to oneself. Any addiction, whether substance or process, has as its main goal that of keeping people out of touch with their feelings and thoughts. When people do not know what they feel and think, they find it absolutely impossible to be honest with themselves.

It is then also impossible to be honest with others, so addicts engage in lying to the people around *them*—the second level. The result is dishonest relationships and, eventually, a dishonest family system.

The dishonest family system then enters the third level: lying to the world. Often, the alcoholic family is perceived as one of the most stable and upstanding in the community. They put on a good front even though chaos reigns at home. Meanwhile, family members are expected to support the lie they live. They get confused and crazy and gradually come to distrust their own perceptions. They lose their ability to distinguish between truth and lying, and the potential for honesty becomes even more remote.

In AA language the addict is a "con." We all know what con artists are: people who will cheat you, lie about themselves and/or the products they are representing, and take advantage of you at the earliest opportunity. Addicts are terrific cons. They are particularly good at figuring out what is appropriate, expected behavior and behaving that way, even when it has nothing to do with who or what they are.

I have seen several skilled cons in my practice. Most were

charming, lovable people who seemed sincere and appeared to be generous and giving; all were liars. They all practiced "impression management," which is telling me what they think I want to hear. Usually they were so out of touch with themselves that they did not realize how dishonest they were being. Lying was the only way they knew to try to control a frightening, overwhelming universe.

Often they also assumed that if they did get in touch with themselves and reveal themselves, nobody would like them. Their dishonesty about themselves was an attempt to control the way others felt about them.

THE THREE "IFS" OF THE ADDICT

Dishonesty in an addictive system reveals itself in the three "ifs" of the addict: *if only, as if,* and *what if.* The "if only" is dishonesty about the past, the "as if" is dishonesty about the present, and the "what if" is dishonesty about the future.

The "if only" signals an attempt to change, control, and lie about the past: "If only my mother had been different, I would have . . ." "If only I had gone to a better school, I would have . . ." "If only I had gotten that break, I would have . . ." "If only" is a way of avoiding dealing honestly with what really happened. When we "if only" the past, we do not have to take responsibility for it or face it, and we cannot learn from it.

"If only" people are out of touch with the way things were; "as if" people are out of touch with the way things are. They are like actors who are perpetually in character.

I know a man who perfectly exemplifies the "as if" personality. He grew up in an alcoholic family and developed almost no identity of his own. He was very bright, had a Ph.D. in psychology, and spent his life trying to act "as if" he were normal. He was so thoroughly invested in his "as if" self that he could not believe that people would like him if they knew the "real" him (whoever that was!).

Our friendship was based upon an unspoken contract: we would both see him the way he wanted to be seen. When I saw him the way he was and liked him anyway, he could no longer tolerate the friendship. I had broken the contract and come too close.

"As if" people can con others into liking them, but they never know whether others are relating to them or to their con, and they cannot risk learning the truth. Because they can never test their relationships, they can never be secure in them.

"What if" people are totally focused upon the future. "What if this happens?" "What if that happens?" In trying to control the future—which is uncontrollable—they mask the present. Dishonesty is apparent in their dealings with themselves and with others and in their expectations of things to come. They are dishonest by not being in the present. They are dishonest in shaping the present to bring about their projected fears.

I have several clients who are at various stages in their recovery from addictions, and one thing is true for all of them: Even the smallest lie or dishonesty will push them back into their disease and threaten their sobriety. There is no such thing as a harmless falsehood.

I used to think that people lied when they were backed into a corner, when they were afraid, when there was some benefit to be gained by lying, or when they had done something they did not want to admit to for some reason. Strangely, those kinds of lying made sense to me; I could see why people resorted to them. What I have since realized is that lying does not have to make sense. Addicts, people raised in addictive family systems, and co-dependents do not need a reason to lie. Frequently they do not know the difference between dishonesty and truth. They may not even know when they are lying.

Some examples from my own experience will demonstrate how ordinary and everyday dishonesty is.

TACOS, PAPERCLIPS, PURSES, AND SHELLS

I had invited a friend for dinner and decided to fix tacos. As I started to prepare the meat, she asked if she could help, so I suggested that she fix the lettuce and the tomatoes. When I turned around, the lettuce was neatly laid out in leaves on a plate, and the tomatoes had been carefully sliced and arranged beside the lettuce.

I said, "That's not how you fix lettuce and tomatoes for tacos." She replied, "I haven't cooked much since my divorce."

What kind of response was that? Confusing, crazy-making, and basically a lie, because it had nothing to do with what I had said.

I might have backed off at that point, but instead I said, "That's irrelevant." To which she countered, "Well, I didn't know how *you* made tacos."

She had done it again! And with my usual tenacity I was not going to let this pass unnoticed. *"Everybody* makes tacos the same way," I insisted. "You're lying. You're covering up the fact that you don't know how to make tacos. So what if you don't know? I don't care. My cat doesn't care. My dog doesn't care. My son doesn't care. My secretary doesn't care. It's all right; you don't have to lie about it. I *do* care about lying."

She puffed up at that, and only later did she admit that I had been right; she *had* been lying. She honestly didn't know how to make tacos, and she had been afraid to admit it.

The entire interaction was enormously convoluted, and one of the two persons involved in it was relatively clear! Imagine what happens when both parties are dishonest! Many of us grew up in families where such exchanges are the norm.

Another friend liked to give intense, emotional, one-syllable responses to questions. Her responses were jolting and confusing. When I said, "How do you like this purple paper clip?" she said, "WONDERFUL."

Now I knew that the purple paper clip did not rate that much enthusiasm, and I also knew that she seldom felt strongly about anything. She was operating so completely out of her addictive behaviors and "ifs" that she was out of touch with most of what was going on inside her.

I followed through. "You're lying," I said. "You don't really feel that strongly about this paper clip. You're saying what you think I want to hear."

Invested in her "as if" personality, she was trying to belong. People around our house tend to be fairly enthusiastic, and she wanted to fit in with the rest of us. What she did not realize was that I would have liked her even if she had *hated* the purple paper clip. I already liked her; I already accepted her—but not because she had controlled or manipulated me into doing it.

Another example: I train mental health professionals in living process therapy. A group of my trainees and I took a trip to the beach. We rode there together in a large station wagon, and when we started back some people changed seats. The woman who had been sitting beside the driver decided to sit behind her instead.

As we drove off, she tapped the person who had taken her place and said, "My purse is under your feet. Give it to me so it won't bother you."

"It's not bothering me," the other woman said. "You can leave it where it is."

"Well, I want to put my glasses in it," the first woman said.

"Hold on," I said to the first woman. "This is a confusing interaction. All you have to say is, 'I want my purse.' You think you're being polite, but you're really being dishonest."

Her dishonesty was subtle. However, she is a recovering alcoholic and cannot afford even the slightest dishonesty. She accepted her dishonesty *and* got her purse.

A final example: Recently I went on a whale watch with several friends and family members. One of my friends felt the need to talk to me, and she decided that the time to do it would be during an afternoon of beachcombing.

She made this decision without consulting me. Had she asked, I would have told her that beachcombing is one of my favorite activities, a time when I relax completely and prefer not to engage in serious talk.

Three of us started off along the beach. My friend stuck close to my side, something I did not think much about at the time. After a while, though, I became aware of a terrible pain in my back. I thought that perhaps I had been stooping too much and tried straightening up, but that did not help. Then I realized that I kept calling the third member of our party back to look at shells I found; I was using her as a buffer. Then I noticed that whenever I walked faster, my friend walked faster, and whenever I slowed down, she slowed down. Then I looked back at our tracks in the sand. I saw that I was zigzagging back and forth across the beach, and that another set of footprints was right beside mine all the way.

I felt drained and "sucked on" and had a backache besides (frequently my body will register something before my mind is fully aware of it). My friend had said that she wanted to join us in shelling when, in fact, she had wanted something else from me. Since I was not aware of her agenda, I was not able to make a choice, and my afternoon was dented, if not ruined. My friend's behavior was controlling and dishonest, and neither of us got what we wanted.

Each of these examples is symptomatic of what happens when people live in addictive systems. My four friends were all recovering and were not engaging in the blatant dishonesty that characterizes the active addict—lying about drinking and drug use, overeating, or affairs—but they still had a long way to go.

Dealing with even small-scale dishonesties is exhausting. Everyone involved must expend enormous amounts of energy simply clarifying interactions. Communication becomes a web of lies. Asking a question when one does not want to know the answer is dishonest. Asking a question when one really wants to make a statement is dishonest. Dishonesty is subtle and universal in our culture.

DISHONESTY AS THE NORM WITHIN THE ADDICTIVE SYSTEM

Everyone who has worked with addicts knows that they have to "get honest" as part of their recovery. Getting honest means getting in touch with one's feelings and dealing with them no matter what they are. As improvement is made in this area (but not before), the addict can move toward being honest with others and the world.

Honesty may be painful and unpleasant at times, but it is never destructive. Dishonesty is always destructive. The Addictive System is built on dishonesty. It is a system in which we are expected to cheat on our taxes and get away with as much as we can. It is a system that teaches that only fools are honest. Women entering the workplace are perceived as naive when they try to be honest. Persons going into management are taught to con. We all learn that we must act "as if" we know something, even when we do not.

I recently became acutely aware of a subtle "lie" that the airlines perpetuate. They say a plane will leave at such and such a time. Now, please do not get me wrong here. Sometimes it is to my advantage that planes leave late, so I do not particularly mind. What I realized is that "on time" and "late" are Addictive System concepts based on a control system. What I became fascinated with was the lie inherent in the airlines' saying when a plane would leave. What they are really saying is that the plane will not leave *before* the designated time. This means that if I want to be sure to be on that plane, I have to be there a few minutes before the designated departure time. Actually, the airlines cannot make a commitment about exactly when a plane will leave. That depends upon the weather, mechanics, baggage, flight schedules, and any number of other things. We accept the basic dishonesty of this statement as normal in the Addictive System, *but* it really is dishonesty. The airlines could be more honest and still get our business, but, unfortunately, they operate on addictive system principles. Of course, this dishonesty is not of major importance; it is important, however, to see how ordinary and acceptable dishonesty is in the system.

On the personal level we learn to lie to avoid "hurting other people's feelings." But that in itself is a lie. What we really care about is not hurting ourselves. We do not want to deal with the consequences of our honesty; we do not want to be confronted with other people's feelings.

About two years ago I attended a reunion with some women I value highly and like very much. We all talked about our work. I shared with them some of what I was doing, how excited I was about it, and how important I felt it was. Two of the women were especially warm toward me and complimented me lavishly. I later discovered that they had talked to a third woman and told her that I had been "tooting my own horn."

Naturally, I was hurt: not so much by their opinion of me (I was saddened by that, and I also thought it was their issue to solve.) What hurt was their dishonesty with me in presenting one face to me and another to someone else.

We see this kind of interpersonal dishonesty throughout our culture. It is particularly apparent in the sexual arena. Most women I know confess to being dishonest in their sexual relationships. They have sex when they do not really want to (and resent it); they fake orgasms to keep their mates happy; and they desperately try to behave the way they think they should.

"Being nice" is another, more insidious form of dishonesty. Some of the sweetest people I have ever met were seething with anger underneath. Niceness in itself is often a form of control. Niceness keeps others from confronting you. In *Women's Reality,* I talked about the Good Christian Martyr, the woman who sacrifices and suffers for others, thereby gaining power over them. It is not surprising that one of the greatest encouragers of niceness is the church.

Dishonesty permeates our political system and our government. After President Reagan was shot, I heard a live broadcast of an interview with the director of the hospital to which he was taken.

I was amazed to hear the doctor answer the questions openly and honestly. He talked about the gunshot wounds, the extent of the wounds, areas of concern, and possible if not probable complications. How exciting to hear the truth. What a rare treat, to get straightforward information out of Washington! I was tempted to wave down other cars on the freeway and say: "Listen to this. You have never heard anything like it." Of course he was never heard from again. From that point on, the White House press corps told the public what it wanted the public to hear.

When we consider our advertising, our businesses, the quality of the materials used in our bridges, and even what our parents tell us about the way life is, we cannot ignore the fact that we live in a system where dishonesty is the norm. We cannot believe what people say. A person's word of honor is as worthless as a drunk's promise to reform. We have systematized dishonesty and assumed it is normal.

ABNORMAL THINKING PROCESSES

Three concepts that are used in chemical dependency circles are worth introducing here: the dry drunk, sobriety, and stinkin' thinkin'.

Dry drunks are people who have stopped drinking and still exhibit all the qualities, behaviors, and attitudes of the drunk. Their thinking processes are the same as if they were still abusing: confused, circular, obsessive, ruminative, and paranoid. They may appear to be psychologically disturbed, frightening, dangerous, and on the verge of violence.

Sober people operate quite differently. They are serene, honest, clear, nondependent, and not self-centered. They have made what I call a system shift; that is, they are no longer operating out of the Addictive System.

Stinkin' thinkin' is an AA term used to describe the addict's abnormal thinking processes. Although these may seem rational and logical within the Addictive System, they almost always make no sense whatsoever. Often they are attempts to "get things back under control"—an illusion—and they are almost always generated out of fear.

People who practice stinkin' thinkin' usually have a hidden agenda. They may want to hide something they have done; they may want to conceal their feelings of discomfort or fear. Instead of taking responsibility for what is going on inside them, they develop a "fog bank"—I also call it an "electron cloud"—of confusing interactions. Their thinking deteriorates, and so do their interactions and relationships.

I once had a recovering alcoholic client whose husband had had an affair. Whenever she slipped into her disease or fell into her dry drunk mode, her thinking became very circular and went something like this: "I know that he is no longer in this affair . . . yet I am afraid that he is lying to me . . . What if he wants to get back into it? . . . What if he is *already* back into it? . . . I drove around for an hour today, trying to find them together . . . I know this is crazy, but I can't stop . . ." She would then ask me, "What do *you* think?"

I would say, "Well I have been seeing him, too, and I know that the affair is over." To which she would reply, "Yes, I know that's right . . . but what if it isn't?"

Left unchecked, stinkin' thinkin' feeds itself forever. It becomes obsessive. People thinking this way go over the same things again and again without ever resolving the issues or getting results. They become even more anxious and stressed. Stinkin' thinkin' is physically and emotionally painful.

Abnormal thinking processes can slip into paranoid thinking processes. As we know, once one accepts the premises of the paranoid delusion, everything *seems* logical and rational—it just makes no sense! Frequently the thinking we see in this system is very logical and rational. It just makes no sense.

Taken to its extremes, stinkin' thinkin' is very similar to schizophrenic thinking. Although I have not yet done much work in this area, I suspect that these two are on a continuum. Perhaps schizophrenia is a result of living in the Addictive System. I suspect so.

It would be interesting to find out how many diagnosed schizophrenics are nonrecovering addicts or members of addictive family systems.

ABNORMAL THINKING PROCESSES IN THE ADDICTIVE SYSTEM

The Addictive System is highly dependent upon what we now call left-brain functions. It is founded on the worship of linear, rational, logical thinking. This kind of thinking supports the illusion of control by simplifying the world to such an extent that it seems possible to have control over it.

White Male System Myth #4 holds that it is possible to be totally logical, rational, and objective. If we believe that, then we must hide from ourselves and others the ways in which we are *not* logical, rational, and objective. This deceit frequently requires us to ignore or dismiss our own experience.

For example, when we live and work within the Addictive System, we spend inordinate amounts of time and energy either going along with, trying to get around, or fighting proclamations from our "superiors" that do not make sense. In my role as a consultant, I have heard quite a few of these statements, and usually they are preceded by certain distinct behaviors.

Whenever a person in a power position is about to make such a statement, (I must admit here that I have found this more prevalent among men in power positions than among women), he will puff up to a greater height (puff, puff, puff). Then he will take hold of and/or adjust his belt and, at the same time, clear his throat. (There appears to be a direct correlation between the length of time spent clearing the throat and the absurdity of the ensuing statement.) By this point, I have figured out that I am in for "one of those," so I brace myself.

Then comes a statement that is really absurd and makes no sense at all: "I am absolutely convinced that the secretaries do better work if they are kept ignorant of the meaning and implications of the projects on which they are typing. If they have too much

information they get emotionally involved and it confuses them."
I wait a few seconds and burst out laughing; the whole perfor-
mance really *is* funny.

After a few suspenseful moments, the man usually unpuffs and
smiles sheepishly. At that point, I say, "That doesn't make any
sense at all, does it?" Most of the time he readily agrees, and we
can move on immediately to a clearer level of communication.

Be warned that this approach is easier for a consultant than an
employee! When one's livelihood depends on superiors who make
no sense, the situation becomes more complicated. In these situations much of the staff's energy must go toward fighting crazy
statements, trying to sidestep or undermine them, or complying
with them against their better judgment. Stinkin' thinkin' has
become our greatest brain drain.

Abnormal thinking processes are especially evident in politics.
Confusion is the norm in political rhetoric. As we listen to
speeches given by our leaders, it is often difficult (if not impossible) to understand what they are saying, not to mention what they
are implying or deliberately leaving unsaid. Innuendos, assumptions, vague statements, planned misinformation, and suggestions
are the stuff of the political world.

ASSUMPTIONS

Stinkin' thinkin' depends upon assumptions to perpetuate itself.
Unclear or confusing statements force one to make assumptions in
order to function. These in turn can lead to further unclear thinking and confusion.

During one of my workshops an incident occurred that illustrates this lack of clarity very aptly. We had baked apples for
dinner. I was too full to eat mine, so I took it back to the cottage
I was sharing with another staff member and put it in the refrigerator, planning to eat it at my leisure. Since it was obviously mine,
it did not occur to me that my cabin mate would eat it.

Later, when I went to get my apple, it was gone. My cabin mate
—a compulsive overeater—had, in fact, gobbled it down. I did not

appreciate that, and I said so. Her response was, "I assumed you didn't want it since you hadn't eaten it."

She had made two assumptions, neither of which she checked out with me: first, that I didn't want the apple, and second, that it was okay for her to eat it. Then she had used her assumptions to support her distorted thinking and feed her compulsive eating habit.

When we live in an addictive system, we use our very good minds to make assumptions that justify what we feel we must do to support our addictions. We fail to see that our assumptions about others have nothing to do with those who will be affected by them, and we do not risk checking them out for fear of what we may find. When reality does not support our confused thinking, we distort reality. This is yet another form of the dishonesty that pervades our culture.

Distorting reality requires that we deny our own experience, the messages our bodies send us, and our inner selves. Our behavior gets progressively crazier, but we *think* we are behaving more logically and rationally. My cabin mate believed that it was logical and rational to assume that I did not want my apple and it was okay for her to eat it. But because her assumptions had no basis in reality, and because she did not check them out with me, she acted on wrong assumptions. At this personal level, this particular interaction had little consequence except to become a good example. Imagine, however, the implications of this kind of behavior on a national or international level.

If we assume that the Russians are going to attack us, it is logical and rational to assume that we must protect ourselves by making the first strike. It is also paranoid. Abnormal thinking processes can and do slip into paranoid thinking processes.

Like many of my colleagues I have become fascinated in recent years with left-brain/right-brain theories and some of their implications for my work. During the early research stages it was believed that the left brain was logical, rational, and linear while the right brain was emotional, intuitive, and nonlinear. Naturally this division proved to be an oversimplification.

Some of my research has suggested to me that the left brain is not entirely without emotion. My experience has shown that the logical, rational mind has one basic emotion, panic. Whenever it is threatened with the loss of its illusion of control, it panics. This panic is a primitive, undifferentiated sort of panic, not nearly as sophisticated or evolved as the emotions produced when the brain is utilized as a whole.

The newest research suggests that the most functional thinking occurs during the synergistic action of both hemispheres and the brain stem. This union produces especially clear and powerful thinking that is far superior to linear, rational thinking. In *Women's Reality,* I described this kind of thinking as "multivariant and multidimensional." What it does is give us a sense of balance, enabling us to check ourselves for distortions, confusion, and dishonesty. We all have this capability, if only we would use it!

However, in a system that functions out of addictive processes, this multivariant thinking is rarely available to us. I want to emphasize here that this kind of thinking is not unavailable just when chemicals are present. In order to move into the clearer multivariant thinking one has to effect a system shift. An addictive system calls forth confused linear thinking.

CONFUSION

I have already said a great deal about confusion as a product of some of the characteristics of the Addictive System. It is also a characteristic in and of itself.

In an addictive system confusion is the norm. Much time and energy are spent simply trying to figure out what is going on. When we are confused, we tend to believe that the world is confused.

When my family and I were living in an addictive household, we were always trying to figure out what was going on. I was often away on speaking engagements and at workshops, and whenever I came home people would line up to complain about and accuse one another.

Using my best family therapy technique, I would call the whole group together to sit down and try to clear things up. (I honestly thought that it was possible to do this.) Playing the role of moderator, I would say, "Now, what did you say to her?" "What did you say to him?" "Did you really say that?" and "Let's get it all out on the table." We believed that all we had to do was communicate more effectively.

At the time we did not realize that this approach was actually making matters worse. When we moved into the confusion to try to clear it up, we became progressively more confused.

When we live in the midst of confusion, we forget what non-confusion is like. People who grow up in addictive households never learn what it is like. Such people (a large proportion of our society) assume that confusion is the way the world is.

In *Women's Reality,* I talked about how women in the Reactive Female System devote themselves to understanding what is going on—with men, with their families, with themselves. (Those who stand *under* have the greatest need to *under* stand.) We see understanding as a way to gain control. But since control is an illusion, our attempts to understand actually often put us deeper into the Addictive System.

THE ROLE OF CONFUSION

Confusion is not just a characteristic of the Addictive System; it also plays a vital role within that system.

First, it keeps us powerless and controllable. No one is more controllable than a confused person; no society is more controllable than a confused society. Politicians know this better than anyone, and that is why they use innuendos, veiled references, and out-and-out lies instead of speaking clearly and truthfully.

Second, it keeps us ignorant. Professionals give their clients confusing information cloaked in intimidating language that laypeople cannot understand. They preserve their "one-up" status while preventing us from learning about our own bodies, our legal rights, and our psychology.

Third, it keeps us from taking responsibility for our own lives. No one expects confused people to own up to the things they think, say, or do, or face the truth about who they are.

Fourth, it keeps us busy. When we must spend all our time and energy trying to figure out what is going on, we have none left over for reflecting on the system, challenging it, or exploring alternatives to it.

These have the combined effect of keeping us stuck within the system. And this, I believe, is the primary purpose of confusion. A confused person will stay within the system because the thought of moving out of it is too frightening. It takes a certain amount of clarity to try new things, walk new roads, and cross new bridges, and confusion makes clarity and risk taking impossible.

One of the best ways to break the pattern of confused thinking is to *stop and wait.* I often tell my clients that important decisions are discovered, not made. Trying to understand does not work. Logical, rational, left-brain thinking does not work. Trying to straighten things out does not work; that only feeds the illusion of control.

People who meditate know the value of stopping and waiting. By sitting quietly and shutting off their left-brain thinking processes, they allow understanding to come to them.

DENIAL

Denial is the addict's major defense mechanism. "I am *not* an alcoholic," the alcoholic says. "I do *not* drink too much. I do *not* have a severe drinking problem. Maybe I have a minor drinking problem, but surely *not* a severe one." Family members—themselves co-dependents and enablers—participate in this denial by putting up a good front to the public. The Addictive System depends on their maintaining the facade of stability and respectability.

Denial allows us to avoid coming to terms with what is really going on inside us and in front of our eyes. I tell my trainees and the people in my workshops to "see what you see and know what you know." The Addictive System does not like this. Seeing what we see and knowing what we know poses a direct threat to it.

When I first became involved in the women's movement, I started to notice things that had never before been apparent to me. Up until then, one of my favorite Sunday-night activities had been watching the Walt Disney television show with my children. We had all been to Disneyland, and the whole Disney enterprise was an important part of our lives.

With my new awareness, I began to see what I was seeing in the Disney shows: how women were portrayed as stereotypes, how they were always stuck in the same roles, and how chauvinistic the story lines were. I had to stop watching them. In some ways, this represented a significant loss for me, but I also knew it was necessary for my own sanity. Continuing to watch would have been a form of self-delusion.

When we refuse to see what we see and know what we know, we participate in a dishonest system and help to perpetuate it. Many women fear the alternative, however. They think that if they see what they see and know what they know, they will no longer be able to relate to the men in their lives (and many other people as well). This may be true to some extent, and fortunately there are some men who are also willing to see what they see and know what they know. These are the men who are choosing to move out of the Addictive System.

We cannot be alive in a system based upon denial. It leaves us no real avenue to deal with our reality.

PERFECTIONISM

It may be hard to picture addicts as conscientious, concerned people with high aspirations and high expectations of themselves, but that is what most of them are. Alcoholics, drug addicts, compulsive overeaters are perfectionists. They are convinced that nothing they do is ever good enough, that *they* are never good enough, that they don't do as much as they should, and that they *can* be perfect if only they figure out how.

Those who treat addicts consider perfectionism to be a major stumbling block to recovery. (The Twelve-Step Program calls it a character defect.) It is difficult to help addicts forgive themselves for not being perfect and perceive themselves as good people anyway. They persist in viewing themselves as *bad* people trying to become good, not as sick people trying to get well.

Being perfect is a real burden. It means always knowing the answers, always having the correct information, always doing everything right, never making mistakes, and constantly reprimanding and beating oneself for falling short. It also means that everyone around the perfectionist has to be perfect. Perfectionists are quite skilled at pointing out other people's flaws!

The Addictive System assumes that it is possible to be perfect. Let us examine how perfectionism relates to the White Male System—Reactive Female System dualism—still more evidence that Addictive System and the White Male System are one and the same.

One of the most striking connections is to the Original Sin of Being Born Female, which I first described in *Women's Reality.* No matter what a woman does, she can never absolve herself of the Original Sin of Being Born Female. Not only does she do things wrong, she *is* a wrong, and she can never make up for that.

The Original Sin of Being Born Female is compounded by the belief in plain old original sin. According to some theologies, this is one of our birthrights. It implies that to be born human is itself a sin.

Now imagine what it is like to be a woman within this system. Having been born both female *and* human, neither of which she can do anything about, a woman is a double wrong from the moment she is born. To be all right, she must become like God as defined by the system. If she can do this she will be "acceptable." Men labor under the same illusion of it being possible to be God. To achieve this God-likeness both men and women have to devalue and relinquish their humanness.

Since we are human, however, it is *not* possible for us to be God, no matter how we define God. We keep trying, and we keep failing, without ever realizing our full *human* potential. The perfectionist exhibits this same compulsive behavior.

The perfectionism of the Addictive System is also related to the second and third myths of the White Male System. Myth #2 states that the White Male System is innately superior. In order to prove ourselves innately superior, we must deny much of who we are. This nonacceptance of ourselves and our humanness supports the illusion of perfectionism.

Myth #3 states that the White Male System knows and understands everything. Many people in our culture spend their lives in hot pursuit of knowing and understanding everything, and of course they never succeed. As women move more into this system, they are taking on the same burden. They are running madly after things they have nothing to do with, know nothing about, and are not even interested in! They are trying to be like white males. Meanwhile they are denying and devaluing what they *do* know. In the same way, addicts (perfectionists that they are) never focus on their good qualities, their virtues, or the knowledge that they have. Instead, they fixate on what they do *not* know, can*not* do, and do *not* understand.

In a system that demands perfection, mistakes are unacceptable. We cannot learn from our mistakes, because we must pretend that we never make any. We must hide them or cover them up.

A client of mine came into group one night with a very interesting story. She had gone to a workshop given by a local psychiatrist and had been impressed with his openness. He had stressed that it was important for men, particularly male psychiatrists, *not* to pretend that they knew everything. My client thought that this was a great step forward, and so did I.

The *way* he put this, however, indicated that he was clear on one level of truth but had not quite moved to the next. "We have to admit that we're not *perfect,"* he said, "and that we make mistakes, and it's okay to admit not being perfect." What he failed to see was that making mistakes *in itself* is a way of being "perfect"—a way of learning, a way of being who we are. To him mistakes were still unacceptable.

Another way that the Addictive System attempts to achieve perfectionism is by defining all things. Something that is not defined by the system cannot (by definition) exist, and if something does not exist one does not have to deal with it. One can choose to deal only with those things that protect one's perfect, all-knowing image. As a result large areas of knowledge remain unavailable or unexplored.

FORGETFULNESS

Forgetfulness is one of the most easily diagnosed characteristics of the addict. It encompasses a wide range of activities and behaviors.

Losing your keys, locking yourself out of your car, locking yourself out of your house, not remembering to pick up the kids at a certain time, not remembering appointments, not showing up for a luncheon date, having things "slip your mind" are all examples of forgetfulness.

On a more serious level is the type of forgetfulness in which you have a conversation with someone and two minutes later do not remember that you committed yourself to doing something, following up on something, or performing some task for a friend or family member.

The most extreme form of forgetfulness is called a blackout. People who black out remember absolutely *nothing* of what they did or said or what was going on around them at the time.

Most of us have had mini-blackouts—times when we are driving down the highway on automatic pilot and realize that we cannot recall having driven a particular stretch of road. These are times of being not present to ourselves. In the addict, these become increasingly severe, until whole days (or even weeks) are lost forever.

People can still function during blackouts; they simply cannot recall anything that happened during them. Blacking out is not the same as passing out. I have heard many stories of alcoholics who have bought airline tickets, flown to other parts of the country (even Europe!), gone about their business, and suddenly come to their senses with no idea of how they got there or what they were doing.

It is important to understand that addicts are not forgetful intentionally; nor are they deliberate liars. When they promise to do something and do not follow through, it is not out of choice. They literally do not remember having made the promise.

When our family was going through treatment in an attempt to understand our disease, our instructor told us something that impressed me deeply. "Since addicts have no memory," our instructor said, "they cannot learn from their experience, because in some ways they have no past." What an appalling thought! It also explains why addicts keep repeating the same behavior time and again. The memory of earlier behavior is unavailable to them— along with anything they might have learned from it.

We have all heard the saying that being ignorant of our history dooms us to repeat the mistakes of our forebears. This seems to be true for persons within the Addictive System. This system is a forgetful, nonlearning system with a selective and distorted memory. It has blacked out the histories of women, blacks, Native Americans, Hispanics, and Asian-Americans. Since those histories are not part of our culture memory, we are doomed to repeat mistakes that could have become opportunities for learning.

The Addictive System does not place much of a premium on remembering the past. To understand why this is the case, we have only to look at a few of the myths. If *this System is the only thing that exists,* if it defines everything and is the only reality, there is no reason to remember anything outside the immediate moment. If *it knows and understands everything,* there is nothing it needs to remember. Finally, if *it is possible to be God,* then remembering is irrelevant, because one is all-powerful anyway.

Besides, forgetfulness is good for the economy. A massive legal system has developed around the need to write things down so people will not forget the agreements they make with one another. Without such documentation to keep them in line, people will distort their agreements. Or, because dishonesty is the norm within the system, they will lie.

When we are confused or off center, when we are not sober, clear, and operating out of our process (to be discussed later), we tend to be forgetful. It is as if large sections of our brains become inaccessible to us. When we are functioning as addicts within the Addictive System, we do not have the learning, information, knowledge, or awareness needed to make reasoned decisions. This is true for the dry drunk as well as the practicing alcoholic or drug user. It is also true for the individual who is addicted to a relationship.

In other words, *any* addictive pattern or process can blur our thinking and block our memory. It causes us to lose contact with what we know and have learned.

DEPENDENCY

Dependency is a state in which you assume that someone or something outside you will take care of you because you cannot take care of yourself. Dependent persons rely on others to meet their emotional, psychological, intellectual, and spiritual needs.

One of my trainees describes dependent people as "human vacuum cleaners." She feels especially susceptible to them because, like most women, she has been taught to be a caregiver. Of course, this is a two-way street: the person who cares for a dependent person is dependent in turn on that person being dependent on her or him. Such a relationship is very tricky and sticky.

Dependent relationships are the norm within the Addictive System.[3] Addicts are almost invariably dependent or counterdependent. Counterdependency has been described in psychological circles as a reaction against extreme dependency. Counterdependent people feel so dependent on others that they must convince them (and the self) that they do not need anyone at all and, hence, act so as to say, "I don't need anybody."

An addict, to recover, must recognize the need to rely on oneself and take care of oneself. Recovery is the realization that one has the ability to do this *and* the ability to stay close to others without being dependent.

This realization contradicts everything we are taught. From an early age we are told that dependency is the road to intimacy, and that two people cannot get close to each other unless they become mutually dependent. Most of our courting is an attempt to establish this interdependency. Two people are deemed intimate when they have reached the stage at which neither can function without the other. We call this the Perfect Marriage.

What I have observed, however, is that dependency *destroys* intimacy. The person being depended upon feels sucked dry, and the person doing the depending comes to resent the other. The relationship that once made both of them feel important and needed and secure eventually leaves them drained and exhausted. Over time they may even come to hate each other. In other words, the mechanism does not work the way we are taught it will work.

Then again, that may be precisely what the Addictive System unconsciously values. I have come to believe that the Addictive System cannot tolerate intimacy. True intimacy requires us to be fully alive and whole in and of ourselves, and this kind of intimacy poses a direct threat to this system. It prefers us to have relationships in which neither person feels secure enough to function independently and to stay in those relationships even after they are long since dead.

THE HOSTAGE-CAPTOR RELATIONSHIP

One of my clients once relayed to me an interesting statement she had heard at an AA meeting: "Alcoholics don't have relationships; alcoholics have hostages." The more I thought about this, the more sense it made.

Hostages do not want to be with their captors. They fear for their lives. They may identify with their captors and take on some of their behaviors (just as a co-dependent takes on the behaviors of the alcoholic), but that, too, is a survival ploy and has nothing to do with intimacy or caring.

I believe that most of the relationships within the Addictive System are hostage-captor relationships. The roles may shift back and forth, with each person sometimes playing hostage and sometimes playing captor, but the dynamic stays the same.

If we look closely, we can see ways in which our family relationships, our business relationships, and our teacher-student relationships are often of the hostage-captor type. In each case the "hostage" does not really want to be there.

Because hostages cannot get what they need from that relationship, they must look outside it. Unfortunately, until there is some recovery, any other relationship the hostage enters into is strictly limited. It cannot begin to meet the hostage's personal or human needs.

The hostage-captor relationship presents a bleak picture, but it is a picture in keeping with the nonliving orientation of the Addictive System. It is precisely the sort of relationship that system encourages.

THE SCARCITY MODEL AND THE ZERO-SUM MODEL

The Addictive System operates out of a scarcity model, a model based on the assumption that there is not enough of anything to go around, and that we had better get as much as we can while we can.

In the section on self-centeredness I gave an example of a mother's behavior toward her young son. I would not be surprised if that boy grew up believing that he had to grab what he could while he could. Already he saw the world as a place where there was not enough of anything for him—even things that were supposed to be his (like his radio and his soft drink). If he wanted something, he would have to grab it and hoard it.

The scarcity model permeates almost every aspect of our lives. We learn to hoard money, material goods, love, and prestige. Because we fear that there is not enough to go around, we accumulate much more than we need or will ever be able to use. (More is better!)

On the individual level this attitude can be relatively harmless; I remember a time years ago when people stockpiled pennies for fear that the supply was running out. On a systemwide level, however, it can be lethal. We currently have so many nuclear weapons that we could never begin to use them all (in the awful event that we would ever use any), yet our military-industrial complex continues to manufacture more each day.

If the scarcity model holds that there is not enough to go around; the zero-sum model postulates that if someone else gets something, it will not be there for me when I need it. Everything is available in limited, finite quantities.

Two examples will help to illustrate these concepts.

I have a group of friends with whom I meet periodically. We are all bright, creative, intelligent, competent people. One of the things I have started noticing is that there is seldom much rejoicing when a person in the group accomplishes something. Why? Because the whole group is operating out of a zero-sum model. If one of the women in it accomplishes something and gains recognition, the belief is that this somehow lessens the amount of recognition available to the other members of the group.

This unfortunate perception has led to a lot of comparing, competing, resentment, and inability to celebrate individual achievements. It has been debilitating for the group and saddening for me, because I know that it limits our capacity for being intimate with one another.

Another example: I have already mentioned that beachcombing is one of my favorite activities. I love to go to a beach to stroll, sit, and gather shells, pebbles, and whatever else I find. There is a beach in Hawaii that I especially like because of its tiny shells. To see them you have to sit for a while and just be quiet; then the shells slowly emerge all around you, embedded in and resting on the sand. If you hunt for them, they elude you.

On one of my trips to that beach, I brought along a friend from Nebraska who is accustomed to wide-open spaces. We sat there together, picking up shells and admiring them. I especially liked the tiny ones, while she preferred those that were larger and more impressive.

We were involved in this activity when a group of Japanese tourists arrived and walked out onto the beach. Suddenly my friend became almost frantic. She jumped up and headed down the beach *ahead* of the group of tourists.

When she returned, I asked her what she had been doing. "I had this overpowering urge to beat them to the shells," she admitted. "I was afraid that they were going to find some that I would have found if I had got there first." We both had a big laugh over this. There were certainly enough shells to go around!

That evening as the sun went down and it became progressively difficult to see the shells in the sand, I started to gather up my things and get ready to return to the beach house. My friend was still picking up shells. I interrupted her concentration and suggested that perhaps it was time to go. "No, just a few more, just a few more," she answered. "I know there are some more here if only I can see them." (By this time, she had to have her nose in the sand to see them at all.)

We talked later that night about what had happened during the day. As it turned out, her behavior had a fairly simple explanation. She comes from a very expansive part of the country. In her mind, big is beautiful and big is important. It took a lot of effort for her to begin valuing the little shells we were finding, and once she did she fell into the scarcity trap. If she did not pick up as many as she could, she would not get what she needed. (Both of us ended up with plenty of shells; four years later, I'm still giving mine away.)

To me this was an interesting example of how quickly and thoroughly we get caught up in the scarcity and zero-sum models. Notice what happens to our behavior when we do!

These models were also operating during the other beachcombing incident I described earlier—the one in which my friend zigzagged along the beach beside me while I developed a pain in my back. She clearly felt that if she did not nail me then and there she might never have another chance to talk to me. She felt that she had to control and manipulate me to get what she needed before time "ran out."

What happens to our relationships when we are driven by these models? We begin to focus on quantity. Sibling rivalry stems directly from the belief that our parents don't have enough time or love to go around. In our sexual relationships we begin to focus on frequency and forget that sex without connectedness is meaningless. Our feelings for our friends and family are colored by jealousy and envy. We want more and more of everything we have; we want what *they* have.

It is easy to see how these models operate in terms of addictions. As a substance or process stops giving us the fix we need (which it always does), we want more and more—more alcohol, more drugs, more money, more gambling, more work, more religion. No matter how much we get, it is never enough. We keep looking outside ourselves for that magical something that will meet our needs and "fill us up."

It is equally easy to see these models at work within the Addictive System. In *Women's Reality* I talked about the differences in how the White Male System and the Emerging Female System perceive and approach the issue of power. In the White Male System power is strictly zero-sum. When *you* have it, I somehow have less of it, and there is only so much to go around. In the

Emerging Female System—the Living Process System—power is perceived as limitless. When I share mine with you, we *both* have more, together and separately.

What is important about power in the Living Process System is that it comes from *inside,* not outside the self. We do not have to look for something external to satisfy our needs. We develop our own strengths and awarenesses and are complete in and of ourselves. The scarcity model simply does not apply.

Compare this to the system in which we live. The Addictive System must continually have more bombs, a larger gross national product, more money, more influence. No matter what we do as a nation and as a society, it is never enough, and it can never make us whole.

NEGATIVISM

Negativism and negative thinking are characteristic of an Addictive System. A necessary part of recovery is becoming aware of how often one perceives oneself, others, and the world in negative terms.

Negativism is directly related to the scarcity model. If you believe that there is not enough of anything, that the world cannot provide for you and you cannot provide for yourself, then it is hard to see your life in a positive way. It is also related to perfectionism. If you are always striving to be perfect, and if you are always (inevitably) falling short of your own expectations, then you cannot feel good about yourself.

Negative thinking is an energy drain that cuts us off from our life force and hastens us toward a nonliving state. Rather than seeing the possibilities within and around us, we see only our limitations and the things we cannot do.

The Addictive System promotes negative thinking. If you accept that *it is possible to be God,* then you are doomed to failure. If you believe that *you can know and understand everything,* then you are doomed to failure. Life becomes a long series of failures, of never quite making it, of perpetually being "one-down" from where you feel you belong.

Consider how the Addictive System goes about the process of analysis. When it examines something closely, it focuses on finding what is wrong with it and picking it apart. We are educated to be critical and judgmental. To be supportive and positive is viewed as being weak. This is especially evident in academia. It is very difficult for academics to consider something and respond to it without feeling that they must come up with something negative to say. Women who are trying to gain acceptance into the academic world notice this and say, "Even when we like something and think it is good, we know that our colleagues will not listen to us unless we find something wrong with it. We have to go out of our way to find something to criticize."

Negativism also spills over into our relationships. Many of my clients claim to have good marriages, but when I ask them what this means, their response is revealing: "He doesn't beat me, he doesn't run around on me, and he doesn't withhold money." What they define as "good" is really the absence of awful! Living within the Addictive System makes it almost impossible to develop a clear concept of goodness.

A new client recently described to me some of the "improvements" she had made as a result of psychotherapy. "I'm not falling apart anymore," she said. "I'm not having bad dreams. I'm not having ineffectual relationships." At this point I stopped her and asked her to listen to herself. None of these so-called improvements was an enhancement to her life; rather, each was a lack of something.

I have a friend who invariably signals when she is about to move into her negative thinking. When she begins a sentence with, "Oh, my Gawd!" I know that she is about to take off into "What if this happens? I hope that doesn't happen. Do you think we did this? Was this fixed? Is this going to work? Are we going to make it?" I start laughing, and she starts laughing, and that is usually enough to shift her out of that perception of the world.

The Addictive System is largely unaware of potential, gifts, excitement, aliveness, or the extravagance that surrounds us and in which we may take joy. The kind of extravagance I am talking about does not cost a great deal of money. Looking out across a bay toward colorful fall foliage and watching ducks float on the water is extravagant. Taking a hot, scented bath is extravagant. Spending time by oneself is extravagant. Simply *being alive* is extravagant! That is what the Living Process System teaches us.

DEFENSIVENESS

Those who work with recovering addicts know that defensiveness is a danger sign, an indication that the addict is moving back into the disease. When one cannot respond to feedback or criticism and instead must prove that one is *right,* no real learning or change can occur.

Defensive people are insecure people. They do not trust their own ability to take in new information, evaluate it, and then accept or reject it. Often they are not even secure about the legitimacy of what they are defending!

It is interesting—and frightening—to see how much defensiveness is a part of our culture. Freud assumed that defense mechanisms were normal and necessary in order to cope with the world. This may be true for the Addictive System; I do not think it is true for the Living Process System. When we live in a system that is compatible with and natural to the human species, a system that accepts us for who and what we are, then we have nothing to be defensive about. In that kind of system all foibles and mistakes are opportunities for growth and learning. When we do not see ourselves in reference to external criteria, we can be more accepting of who we are.

DENIAL AND PROJECTION AS DEFENSE MECHANISMS

I have already discussed the role of denial as a defense mechanism. It is important now to recognize that the Addictive System does not see it as such. Instead, it views denial as a normal way of being in the world.

As long as we refuse to see what we see and know what we know, we can accept that system and actively support it. When we lower our defenses and start trusting our own perceptions, we become a threat.

Projection is a form of denial. Rather than deal with our own feelings, we project them onto others. This is especially apparent in the paranoid. Rather than deal with their own anger and hostility, paranoids project them out onto those around them, frequently strangers. Paranoids see *them* as angry, hostile, and ready to attack—and respond to them accordingly. In the most extreme cases, paranoids will kill another person out of a belief that person is about to kill them.

Whenever we make assumptions about others and then act on those assumptions, we are skipping a crucial step in the thinking process: *checking out* our assumptions. Paranoids have bought into the Addictive System so thoroughly that they have forgotten how to perform this step.

Several years ago, when I lived in New York City, I spent a lot of time on public transportation. I would often give my seat on the bus or subway to an older woman. What usually happened was that the woman would take the seat and then stare at me for the rest of the ride, holding her purse tightly. One woman watched me for about fifty blocks before getting off. As she stood up, she said to me, "Thank you, dearie, I've never seen anyone do that in New York before."

The longer I lived in New York, the more I realized that paranoia was the norm there. Being perpetually defensive was considered to be a survival skill. You simply assumed that everyone would try to hurt you and behaved as if it were true.

What happens when we live defensively—the way the Addictive System wants us to live? We rob ourselves of the potential to learn. We close ourselves off to information that could move us to new levels of awareness and a new understanding of ourselves. We stop growing.

What happens when we are defensive system-wide? We have only to look at our Addictive System government to find the answer to that question. As a nation, we are obsessed with proving we are *right*. That in turn results in our being unwilling to negotiate and unable to grow. We are so busy trying to *know and understand everything* that we must hide any uncertainty and cover up the fact that we do not have all the answers. We bluster, we bully, and meanwhile we fear for our lives.

COMMUNICATION AND COUNTERCOMMUNICATION

"Addicts don't communicate; they interrogate"—was another interesting statement heard at an AA meeting. I once counseled a husband and wife for whom this was a real problem. He was a recovering alcoholic. She was concerned about their ability to work things out because, as she told me, "We can't communicate." It so happened that he was a police officer, and he talked to her in the same way he talked to criminal suspects. He would ask the questions—"What have you been doing? What do you think? What do you feel about this? What's going on here?"—and she would provide the answers. At the end of each so-called attempt at communication, she felt as if she had been interrogated under a glaring light.

This kind of communication does not lead to bridging. It leads to defensiveness, secrecy, and fearfulness. The end result is *counter* communication, a confusing, convoluted exchange in which nothing positive can occur.

There are several reasons why countercommunication is the norm within the Addictive System. First, addicts do not want to communicate directly, openly, or honestly, because to do so leaves them vulnerable and exposed. It is easier—it is preferable—to keep everyone around them confused. Second, addicts *cannot* communicate clearly, because their thinking is so unclear. Often they really do not know what they are thinking and feeling. Third, the Addictive System teaches that it is good to confuse and intimidate others, because this is one way to gain the upper hand and maintain the illusion of control.

There is little if any understanding that communication can be used to bridge information gaps between two separate human beings. This is partly because addicts do not even perceive others as separate from themselves. The lack of ego boundaries (pseudopodic ego) results in their perceiving everything as themselves; everything and everyone else becomes ME.

RESPONSIBILITY AND BLAME

Addicts characteristically avoid taking responsibility for themselves and their lives. I have worked with many recovering addicts, and I believe I know one reason for this unwillingness. They equate responsibility with blame. If they are responsible for what has happened in their lives, then they must be to blame for it all, and everything that has befallen them is their fault.

The Addictive System places great emphasis on cause-and-effect, which, of course, is closely related to the illusion of control. "If something has happened to me," the perception goes, "it is because I made it happen. I believe that I can and should be in control, therefore I must have been in control, and therefore I have done this to myself."

One of the most important shifts that occurs in the recovering person is the movement away from this perception. The healthier one becomes, the more clearly one sees the difference between responsibility and blame. Taking responsibility for one's life means *owning* it, not controlling it. It is only when we own our lives, our feelings, and our experiences that we are able to learn from them and embark on the healing process.

I have a friend who used to work with me on various projects. We saw each other infrequently, and whenever we got together she insisted that we sit down and discuss the problems she felt she was having with me. *I* was not having any specific problems with *her*, but I was willing to go along with her need to talk. When we did, she always began by saying that I had to take 50 percent of the responsibility for the problems between us.

Now, I am well trained in traditional psychological therapy, and I used to buy into the belief that when one person was having problems with another, the two of them ought to share the responsibility. So I would sit with my friend at length, listen to her accuse me of various things, and promise to look closely at each of the problems she claimed to be having with me. During these interactions, I often felt confused. I could not understand why we were talking about these things, or why she kept telling me to take 50 percent of the responsibility when that was what I always did.

When our talks were over, I would always believe that we had worked things out between us. I would go off by myself and review the conversation, checking for anything that seemed unfinished. Were her accusations valid? Did they match my experience? Then I would deal with my feelings about the interaction, take responsibility for my part in it, and consider the case closed. By the time of our next meeting, I would be excited about seeing my friend—and she would start the whole thing over again!

This happened so often that I started calling it the "50 percent solution." I also started realizing that this was a misnomer. She and I had never shared responsibility equally. I would take on my half of it, sort through it, get clear, let it go, and come back to the relationship believing that everything was settled and no old feelings were hanging around. My friend, on the other hand, would come back to it carrying the same old feelings, resentments, and grudges. She would not do the interim work of assuming her own share of the responsibility for what was happening between us. In other words, my 50 percent solution was actually a 75 percent solution; I was carrying the bulk of the burden.

This happens all the time in the Addictive System. Those who are willing to do their own work within a relationship end up with 75 percent of the responsibility then 85, and so on. Meanwhile, the other person does not even take care of the 25 percent that is left behind.

Several years ago my then husband (now ex-husband) and I went into therapy together to try to solve the difficulties we were having in our relationship. The psychiatrist we saw was someone we also knew professionally. Before long, the three of us realized that my husband was the one who usually made the opening gambit for a fight. The second move was mine. The psychiatrist took the position that it was my responsibility *not* to make that move, since I saw the game for what it was.

I maintained that this approach was not fair. It gave me total responsibility for the relationship. What about also asking my husband not to make the *first* move? Why did one person have to do it all? We quit therapy soon after that. The therapist (who happened to be male) and my ex-husband were operating out of the same system, and I was outnumbered.

We have distorted the concept of joint responsibility. We say that it means a sharing, fifty-fifty, but that is seldom the case. When one person keeps taking 50 percent of what's there and the other does not do any personal work, the percentage increases in a geometric progression. It is easy to see why the balance shifts. When we equate responsibility with blame, we naturally do not want any part of it.

TUNNEL VISION

I first noticed what I call the tunnel vision of the Addictive System in a man I know who was raised in an alcoholic family and has many of the characteristics of an alcoholic. Whenever he focused his attention on me, I felt like a queen, as if I were the center of love and affection and nothing else mattered but me. At the time this illusion felt wonderful. (Later I realized that this was what I had been taught to believe *real* love was all about. *Real* love involved that level of attention and intensity of focus.)

Things changed the moment he shifted his gaze, however. When he looked away from me, it was as if I ceased to exist for him, as if there were no threads or connections that bound us together beyond the moment of eye contact.

Then I noticed that precisely the same thing happened with other people (especially women) when they were in his presence. As soon as he turned to them, they reacted just as I did. Each felt like a queen, as if she were the most loved person in the world, and then, suddenly, he was gone.

The picture became crystal clear when his grown daughter came for a visit. I was very excited about meeting her and getting to know her. But when the three of us were together, it was as if only two of us could relate at any given time, the man and I or the man and his daughter. Meanwhile, the other stood by on hold. Whenever he talked with her, I ceased to exist for him; whenever he talked with me, she faded into the background. Each of us felt abandoned when we were not the center of his focus.

As a result she and I began to feel as if we had to compete for his attention. There was not enough of it to go around (scarcity model!). I did not want to feel that way, yet I could hardly stop myself; his tunnel vision elicited powerful competitive tendencies in me. Fortunately his daughter and I were able to talk about it, and we refused to play the game.

I started identifying this tunnel-vision characteristic in the addicts with whom I worked. It almost always had the effect of limiting the amount of contact they had with other people. Tunnel vision does not permit much interaction, because the person who has it can focus on only one person at a time. It makes it virtually impossible to maintain several different connections simultaneously, which is basically how relationships have been set up in our society.

A childhood friend and I discussed this phenomenon not long ago. The two of us grew up together, and although we now live quite far from each other we have reconnected as adults. On one of his visits, I said to him, "When we're apart, I feel as if I cease to exist for you. But I want you to know that it doesn't happen the other way around. I feel that there are always threads binding us together in a positive, caring way. There are times when these threads are stretched thinner because we're not in touch, but they're still there regardless of whether we write letters or call or see each other. They are always there for me."

This came as a new idea to him, and he found it fascinating. Ever since, he has been trying to develop this feeling of sustained connection, even when we have no contact at all, and he reports that he has been thrilled by the outcome of his experiment.

Tunnel vision is inherent to the Addictive System. When we are operating out of an addictive system, if we focus on one thing only, nothing else exists for us. As a result, we do not make or maintain other connections, whether interpersonal, spiritual, intellectual, or emotional. This way of doing things also exists at the societal level. We focus on one idea, one person, or one country, and other ideas, persons, and countries cease to exist for us or are a threat to our focus, our "reality." There is something exciting about that intensity, yet it has an unreal and destructive quality.

Another notable effect of tunnel vision comes from its need for intensity. Often addicts are so out of touch with their feelings that they feel dead and unable to respond to the world. They then create situations for themselves that are almost superhumanly intense; they may even reach crisis proportions. In the process they feel alive, however briefly. But as their addictions progress and they become more and more dead inside, they seek increasingly intense feelings because the lesser ones no longer register.

This dilemma is especially evident in Addictive System relationships. There is always the search for the new thrill, the higher level of intensity, and what usually happens is that this intensity gets confused with intimacy or reality. Intensity itself becomes a fix.

FROZEN FEELINGS

There is a term in alcoholic circles that applies equally well to the Addictive System: *frozen feelings.* Understanding it is essential to understanding the entire addictive process.

From working with addicts we have learned that they tend to be almost totally out of touch with their feelings. Treatment professionals know that they must help addicts to reestablish some kind of connection with their feelings, some awareness of what those feelings are. This connection may be tenuous or even superficial at first, but it must be made.

Interestingly, addicts are often persons who feel very intensely; they are just incapable of dealing with their feelings in a healthy way. Addictions function to shut off, block out, and push down those feelings that addicts believe they cannot handle: fear, anger, anxiety, panic, rage, even joy, excitement, pleasure, and contentment. Furthermore, addicts have almost no ability to differentiate among their feelings. Fear, anger, and anxiety seem to feel the same, if, in fact, they are felt at all.

If we think about our culture and the parenting practices used to raise most of us, it becomes evident that the emphasis is on controlling ourselves and controlling our feelings. Recall how Jackie Kennedy behaved at her husband's funeral. The president's brains had just been blown out, and Jackie looked as if she had been drugged. She stood there impassive, stoic, trying not to shed a tear, and this image was held up to us as the ideal of American womanhood.

Our movies, newspapers, and television programs tell us that we must never show our feelings. Men in particular are taught not to show their feelings from a very early age, which is probably why they are better at it than women. (This may be one reason why our society perceives men as superior beings.) People who feel are a threat to the system, whether they feel angry, happy, hateful, contented, vindictive, or joyful. It does not matter whether a feeling is negative or positive; we must keep it locked inside.

By robbing us of the freedom to experience and reveal our feelings, the Addictive System robs us of important information about who we are. It also robs us of life; repressing our feelings long enough can eventually kill us. (Recent studies have shown that the tears we cry when peeling an onion are not the same chemically as those we cry out of emotion; the latter actually drains poisons out of the body.)

I never cease to be amazed at the number of people who come to me for therapy or show up at my workshops without having any idea of what they are feeling. One couple stands out in my mind: During the first interview, the man was obviously overcome with a feeling over and over again; I could almost see it shudder through his body. Each time I would stop and ask, "What was that? What were you aware of? What were you feeling?" And each time he would reply, "Nothing. I wasn't aware of anything."

At the end of that session he asked if he could begin individual therapy with me. He said that he was feeling out of touch with what was going on inside him, and that I was the first therapist who had even noticed that something was happening. Over the next year or so, as he became more aware of his feelings, he realized that he was gay, had always been gay, and had repressed that knowledge in order to fit into a "normal" marriage. It was killing him psychologically and physiologically. In time he was able to discuss this with his wife, and they mutually agreed to divorce. Each has since been able to adjust, and both are much happier.

We use our addictions to block our feelings without understanding why. Most people who find themselves craving a drink, a cigarette, or a snack when they feel anxious do not connect the craving with the anxiety. They feel something that they cannot label and do not comprehend, and they head for their ingestive or process fix. The more dead inside they become, the more they must heighten the intensity of their feelings in order to feel anything at all. They set up situations for themselves of extreme anger, pain, or fear just to remind themselves that they are alive.

I recently worked with a woman who has been recovering for several years. The first addiction she discovered was alcohol, and after going through treatment for that she began working on other addictions, including co-dependence, food, and cigarettes. Not too long ago she attended one of my workshops. At first she claimed that she was not feeling anything. Then she stopped and said, "Wait. That isn't true. I think I am feeling something—contentment! I never knew what it was, and I never labeled it before, and it's so subtle that I didn't even know it *was* a feeling!"

When we live in the Addictive System, our feelings are seen as liabilities. We are not allowed to experience, express, or discuss them. Only by moving out of that system can we begin to function fully as whole persons with a range of emotions and intuitions. Only by moving out of that system can we truly begin to live.

ETHICAL DETERIORATION

A concept that is key to understanding the Addictive System and what it is doing to us is ethical deterioration.

Those of us who treat addicts quickly learn to recognize the signs of ethical deterioration or "spiritual bankruptcy." It is easy to see that severe alcoholics or drug addicts are no longer in touch with their ethics or spirituality. They will steal, lie, and in extreme cases even murder for their fix. It is not as easy to see that these behaviors make up a continuum. Ignoring or mistreating one's children, failing to pay one's bills on time, being dishonest within relationships, cheating on one's taxes are all symptoms of the same thing. They are all related.

I believe that each of us carries inside some very clear ideas of what is right for us, and what, for us, would be evil—a personal morality. We *know* when we are lying, or being selfish, or hurting someone, or doing something we should not do. The Addictive System invites us to compromise our personal morality at every turn. Furthermore, it gives us all the tools we need to do so. Self-centeredness, the illusion of control, abnormal thinking processes, denial, defensiveness, fear, frozen feelings, and each of the other characteristics of that system are handed to us as ways to avoid being moral, responsible persons. They silence the voice inside us that speaks the truth. On a national level, we come to believe that what we do is right because *we* do it.

At a deeper level, the Addictive System enables us to deny our spirituality. We lose contact with the awareness that we are spiritual beings with important spiritual connections. I want to make it clear that I am not talking about religion. I am talking about *spirituality,* and the two can be quite different. In fact, there are many ways in which religion may cause us to deviate from our spiritual base.

The loss of our spirituality plunges us into addictive functioning. What happens is that the Addictive System creates God in its own image and then distorts that image to suit its own purposes. This is an integral part of the delusionary nature of the system. That distortion further separates us from our spirituality and our awareness of ourselves as spiritual beings.

The Addictive System assumes that you will cheat on your income taxes. If you do not, you are seen as naive. It assumes that you will be dishonest in your business dealings. If you are not, you are seen as unsophisticated. It assumes that you will try to hoard more than you need. If you do not, you are seen as someone who is not functioning properly within the system.

People who refuse to be dishonest in order to advance their careers and get more power and more money are often told that they are "not aggressive enough" or "not ambitious enough." They are told that they do not know how to "make it" in the system. There is little or no recognition that they are functioning within a *different* system.

I have come to believe that the loss of spirituality makes us dangerous to ourselves and others. I have also come to believe that spirituality cannot be approached only through the left brain. Left-brain theologies teach us to rationalize, objectify, and be logical about our spiritual selves. The trouble is that spirituality has nothing to do with rational, objective, logical thinking. It has to do with the *experience* of the spiritual self, which tends to be irrational, nonobjective, and illogical.

Addictions remove us from that experience by blocking it and making it inaccessible to us. What I have found in working with known addicts, and also with people who are not considered to be addicts but have been reared in the Addictive System, is that they have become progressively out of touch with their spiritual selves. What I have tried to do in all cases is to help them take the first, tiny steps toward reconnecting with their spirituality. This is often a slow and painful process. It is never brought about through purely rational or logical thinking and seldom through following the dictates of an organized religion.

It is becoming progressively more difficult to deny that we live in a system in which lying, cheating, and stealing are the norm and in which these behaviors are justifiable simply because they support the system. Even mass murder is justifiable if it supports the system. We see all around us—and feel inside us—the price we are paying.

When we offer up our spiritual beings to perpetuate the system, we participate in our own movement and our society's movement toward nonliving. To be spiritual means to embrace being fully alive, and to be alive means to be spiritual.

FEAR

The Addictive System is based on fear. We fear for our very survival, and our children grow up fearing for theirs. In a system that fosters violence and uncertainty, where confusion and self-centeredness are rampant, where the scarcity model dictates that there is often not enough food, money, time, or energy (because of *actual* hoarding), healthy survival is a very real concern.

Almost all the characteristics of the Addictive System I have described thus far are rooted in fear. The illusion of control, crisis orientation, dishonesty, abnormal thinking processes, denial, dependency, negativism, defensiveness—each is born out of fear. When we do not know our own boundaries, when we perceive the world as either for or against us, when we never have enough of anything, we cannot help but be fearful. The only way we can hope to survive is by controlling what others think, do, and say and minimizing their effect on us.

Fear makes us dependent upon our addictions. In a system in which the possibility of total annihilation is ever present, addictive substances or processes serve to block our awareness of our terror. Alcohol, drugs, food, and television also make us numb to our own reality—to seeing what we see and knowing what we know. We keep generating crises for ourselves, which guarantees that we always feel a threat to our survival. And this threat, of course, further strengthens our dependency on our addictions, on the regular fixes that give us the illusion of being in control of our lives.

Fear permeates the Addictive System. Women in the Reactive Female System are always fearful because they believe that they cannot exist without male validation and approval. When you believe that you are not a legitimate human being in and of yourself, and that your legitimacy hinges on outside validation and approval, you live in constant fear. You are uneasy about trusting your own perceptions and feelings, because there is always the chance that they will differ from those of the people who give you legitimacy. When they do in fact differ, it feels like psychological annihilation.

Fear is what holds the Addictive System together. The system could not survive without it.

THE ADDICTIVE SYSTEM AS AN ILLUSIONARY SYSTEM

I have come to see the Addictive System as an illusionary system. I arrived at this by an interesting route. I did not see it for a long time, and then one day it became crystal clear.

I had read Richard Bach's *Illusions,*[4] and I had studied many of the Eastern beliefs that "all is illusion." I had watched this concept take hold in many spiritual circles, and for me there was something intrinsically wrong with it.

Then one day I was driving through the Colorado mountains with the top down on my car, pondering the notion that we create our own reality and that everything is an illusion. I was looking at the mountains when suddenly I realized the folly of that idea. *I* had not created those mountains. All the intelligent, clear-thinking people I knew could not have created those mountains, yet they were there. The system most certainly had not created those mountains, and, indeed, they had nothing to do with the system. They were, themselves, a reality.

The Addictive System defines itself as reality and everything else as nonexistent (nonreality). It requires that we ignore our reality and our experience, deny what we see and what we know, and define the world according to its terms. Since it itself is illusionary, it asks us to perceive *everything* as illusion. But that in itself is an illusionary action, reflective of an illusionary system.

Let me say more: since the Addictive System is itself an illusionary system, it defines everything according to its reality, which is illusion, and, therefore, says that *all* is illusion. The Addictive System is based upon the illusion of control, the illusion of perfectionism, thinking processes that twist reality into left-brain constructs, dishonesty, and denial. The belief that the Addictive System itself is the only reality is itself an illusion that moves us to believe that there is no reality. There is, however, reality, and we know it through our participation in our clear experience. This is what I call the Living Process System. We have moved away from our knowledge, our awareness of reality, and our perceptions in order to fit in.

This illusionary system is not only a convoluted thinking process and an elaborate system of defenses; it is also a lot of nonsense!

To maintain our illusions and live in an illusionary system, we must shut off reality in as many ways as possible. That is why addictions are essential to the survival of the Addictive System. Addictions keep us from seeing what we see and knowing what we know. They enable us to fit comfortably into a system that is nonliving, a system in which mountains become figments of the imagination.

SUMMARY

In this section I have attempted to explore some of the more common known characteristics of the addict and demonstrate how these same characteristics operate on a systemic level. As I stated earlier, this is a holographic concept. The individual reflects the system and the system reflects the individual. They are the same and different simultaneously. We see exactly the same characteristics operating in the system as we see in the individual addict.

In order to understand the system in which we live and help move it toward recovery, the time has come to admit, without reservation, that it is an addict and functions on a systemic level the same as any decompensating or deteriorating drunk. We must move beyond our participation in this disease process, beyond our denial, and see the elephant in its context for what it is, an Addictive System.

III. PROCESSES OF THE ADDICTIVE SYSTEM

INTRODUCTION

In Part II, I talked about characteristics of the addict and the addictive system. I also discussed process addictions. In this part I shall explore the major processes of the Addictive System and their implications. Later I shall explore the concept of life process and living in process.

I realize that it can be confusing to use the word *process* in three ways. Yet, paradoxically, and holographically all three are the same *and* different.

By labeling certain addictions process addictions, we are able to distinguish them from ingestive addictions. Process addictions are unhealthy and destructive ways of being in the world. They lead to perceptions and behaviors that are growth-inhibiting, counterproductive, painful, and even death-producing. In the beginning these processes may seem satisfying or pleasing to us, but once we become hooked they no longer serve their original purpose. Our joy in work moves into working compulsively. We make money not only to meet our needs but because we are driven to make money.

What I mean by the processes of the Addictive System will become clear in this part of the book. Before I go on, I want to say a few words about life process and living in process, the third way in which I use the term *process.* I believe that each of us has a healthy process that is our own life process. You have a life process that is distinctly yours, and no one can live it but you. When you do, you feel happy and serene and your life is "working" for you. Living your process is living in tune with your own inner guidance, awareness, integrity, spirituality, and morality. It is living in tune with yourself as you really are.

Any system has its contents, roles (definitions), and processes. Depending on its orientation, it may emphasize contents over processes, or roles over contents. Because the Addictive System is oriented toward control, it focuses mainly on contents and roles. The assumption is that if we change the contents, everything else will fall into place.

Behavior modification and other similar types of therapy are based on this assumption. They teach that if we change the way we think or act, or if we learn something new, then we do not have to deal with our own processes at all. If we give people a new set of facts, then they will change their behavior accordingly. Many expensive management workshops are founded on this belief. People go to them expecting to learn certain things; they are taught those things (and given lots of handouts); and everyone goes away thinking that something important has been accomplished.

Processes are more difficult to name and change, and they are far more powerful than contents. For example, consider what happens when a mother tells her child, "I am NOT angry!!" Now, the *content* of this message is that the mother is not angry, but the *process* is that she is very angry indeed. The child can tell this from her tone of voice, the expression on her face, and her posture. And the child thinks, "Of course Mom is angry. Why is she saying she isn't?" (When we send our children this kind of mixed message, we are encouraging them to believe they are crazy!)

Thus far we have named the *contents* and *roles* of the Addictive System—the *whats*. Now it is essential to name its processes—the *hows*. They are the secret strengths of the system; they are what perpetuate it; and up until this moment they have gone essentially unnamed.

THE PROCESS OF THE PROMISE

The Addictive System is built on the process of the promise. There is very little (if any) difference between the two statements "I will quit drinking tomorrow" and "A chicken in every pot." Both keep us looking expectantly toward the future and not recognizing, owning, and dealing with the present.

There is no group in our society more adept at this process than the church, for which one of the major premises is that of eternal life. That promise keeps us actively involved in pleasing the church and doing what it tells us to do. We ignore the present because we are assured salvation and a brighter future. We can look to a time when our worries and cares will fall away and be replaced by bliss—so why change today?

The promise of the Addictive System is that *it is possible to have everything* we want and need as long as we accept and conform to the system. We grow up believing that any of us can be wealthy, win the lottery, or be president someday. We keep trusting the system to take care of us.

The promise of the Addictive System is that *things are going to get better.* Someday our partner is going to quit drinking or doing drugs. Someday our partner is actually going to do the psychological work she or he needs to do in order to get well. Someday our partner is going to get a job or pay off her or his debts. Battered wives who stay with their abusive husbands honestly believe them when they say, "I'll never do it again." They buy the promise.

Whenever I work with addictive families, one thing that invariably arises is the fear of holidays and special occasions. Holidays always hold the promise of being special times, warm times, family times, but that promise is broken again and again. For most people from addictive families, holidays are especially miserable. Yet they keep expecting things to get better! They refuse to deal with the reality of what holidays are like for them. This refusal in turn creates tension and stress, which is usually relieved by creating some sort of crisis.

The process of the promise is often what keeps addictive relationships going. The focus on the future keeps everyone static and mired where they are. No one can escape the system, and no one can heal. In order to continue to believe in the process of the promise, one must develop an increasingly elaborate denial system and continue to deny one's experience.

One of the things I see happening in our culture at present is a breakdown of this process. Operating out of a scarcity model, we have hoarded until a lack of resources, energy shortages, and worldwide food shortages are forcing us to wonder how much longer we can continue to be deluded with the promise of abundance.

THE PROCESS OF ABSORPTION/PSEUDOPODIC EGO

Another process the Addictive System uses to perpetuate itself is that of absorption. The pseudopodic ego of the system reaches out and totally absorbs another system until it becomes indistinguishable from the Addictive System. It is similar to colonization, a favorite practice of the Addictive System down through history.

Let me illustrate with an example from my own life. I have been friends with a certain man for many, many years. He frequently comes to visit and stays at our house for a week or so. Once I asked him why, and what he seemed to get out of it, since he spent most of his time just hanging around and not doing anything special. He replied, "You have a very healing household, and I come out to get in touch with myself and get my needs met."

I replied, "I'm not surprised that you don't get your needs met where you live and work, because it's impossible for a community that is dishonest and controlling to meet human needs." (I had been there in a consulting capacity, and I knew what it was like.)

He became quite defensive. "You're wrong about it," he said. "You were there under special circumstances, and you didn't see it the way it really is."

I was not surprised to have what I said dismissed, especially by a man. It usually begins when they are able to object to or disprove some small part of my reasoning. They then use that to feel justified in dismissing the rest of what I am saying. This also is a technique often used by the Addictive System. When we do not want to face our addictive disease, we find something wrong with any small part of what a person is saying, then dismiss everything that is being said; in so doing we "protect our supply," as they say in AA.

Many years ago I would have withdrawn, gone away, and never returned to the issue. Right after I became a feminist I would have come out fighting and angrily resisted being dismissed. At this point in my development, however, I was able to step back, recognize the process that was going on between us, and name it.

"I'm not going to let you use this ploy to dismiss me," I said. "You're right about my being there under special circumstances. But that has nothing to do with my perception and does not mean that my observations are invalid."

He grudgingly agreed that my perception was true, and we were able to proceed with our discussion. "It's true that I usually don't get my needs met there," he said, "but every once in a while the people in my community come through. Someone's parent dies, or something bad happens to someone, and people come through for them."

I suddenly realized that what he was talking about was a *systems shift.* He was referring to times when another system had broken through—a system that was not dishonest or controlling, a system that was totally different from the Addictive System. The Addictive System had simply absorbed and claimed this shift as its own and named it as part of its own system.

The same thing has been happening to Living-Process-System people down through the ages. Whenever we "come through" with something the Addictive System needs—a clarification, for example, or a healing, or caring or honesty or gentleness—the pseudopodic ego of that system absorbs it and uses it to perpetuate itself. Ironically, it is these infusions of life from the Living Process System that keep the Addictive System going in spite of itself! These processes are used to infuse the Addictive System and are owned by it. This perpetuates the system just as the co-dependent keeps the alcoholic going.

Like the process of the promise, the process of absorption may be seen at work in many addictive relationships. When we ask people why they stay in these destructive relationships, their response usually goes something like this: "I know that things are really terrible, but once in a while—every few months, or even once a year—something different happens. We communicate, or something else changes, and I start believing we can make it." In other words, another system breaks through. And because it is something the Addictive System needs at that point in time, it is absorbed by that system, becomes indistinguishable from it, and is used to perpetuate it.

The Addictive System also deals with differences by making them nonexistent. A black person is not really a black; he or she is "just like us." This denial is yet another example of absorption and the pseudopodic ego at work.

For instance, the following appeared in a 1985 article in *The New York Times:*[1]

> Jarvis Stanford, a twenty-year-old black man, works with Allan Shenberger in the Kroger store. "Al and I get along real good," he said. "Sometimes I go over to the gas station. Sometimes he comes over here and we sit and rap and listen to my James Ingram tapes." About Stanford, Shenberger said: "Jarvis is great. To me, there are blacks and there are niggers, but I'd have to say Jarvis is white. We have a good time with each other. He's brought me out of the dumps many times."

Need I say more?

THE PROCESS OF ILLUSION

As I said earlier, the Addictive System is an illusionary system. Using itself as the criterion, it defines everything else—all of our experience and our reality—as an illusion.

At best, this is confusing; at worst, it is paralyzing. Our questioning, feeling, exploring brains are being held captive by our rational minds.

We are told that the illusion—the ability to be God, to know and understand everything, to be always logical and rational, and to be superior and in control—is real. This sets up a conflict between perceived reality and illusion. To resolve it, we use our rational, logical thinking processes (analysis and intellectualization) to elevate the unreal to the real and develop mechanisms to explain and correct for this. We dismiss our experience and our reality as invalid. This dismissal, in turn, has the effect of removing us even further from our experience and our reality—and so it goes.

For example, I have learned that it is not my logical, rational mind that tells me when I am being lied to. It is my solar plexus. Last year, during the national elections, I had the opportunity to listen to and see our national leaders on television. I was told that I was being told the truth, what was being said was rational and logical. Yet my solar plexus disagreed. Had I been relying on addictions to suppress my feelings, I would not have been aware of my visceral response, but I *was* aware of it. In order to believe the person on television, I would have had to dismiss my own awareness and reality, declare them invalid, and buy the illusion. I could not ignore myself in this way.

I believe that the constructs of the linear, rational, logical brain, while interesting, are almost completely unrelated to our experience of ourselves and the world. Yet these are what we keep telling ourselves are real.

One of the offshoots of the process of illusion is the illusion of control. We have already described the *whats* of this process; now let us examine the *hows*.

We live in a system founded on the belief that it is possible to control ourselves, other people, other systems, other countries, even the universe. We spend much of our time, energy, and money pursuing this illusion. We then spend equal amounts cleaning up the resulting mess. Our physical bodies suffer so much stress when we try to control our own feelings and emotions that it erupts in high blood pressure, ulcers, colitis, heart attacks, and strokes. Our relationships with other people fail because we try to control everyone with whom we come in contact. Our planet is on the brink of disaster because of the elaborate and lethal defense systems we have created in attempting to control other nations.

A person or a system that lives in process knows that it is totally impossible to exert that kind of control. Such a person or system does not even try, because it sees control for the illusion it is.

THE PROCESS OF THE EXTERNAL REFERENT

The process of the external referent is the basic process of self-definition in the Addictive System.

This process requires us to develop our concept of self through external referents. A woman who believes she is guilty of the Original Sin of Being Born Female must seek approval and validation from outside, usually from a man, before she can have an identity. In this system, the self is established externally. We are what our families, our schools, the church, and various other institutions say we are.

We learn to judge our successes by how other people judge them. We learn to give up our awareness of the messages inside ourselves that tell us what we feel or think. We respond to situations according to what is expected of us.

We do not just seek information and feedback from the people around us; we let them determine who we are. Our point of reference is outside ourselves.

One of my friends recently accompanied me to a conference. She did not attend most of the meetings, including the one where I spoke. Even though the topic was of interest to her, she decided that what she needed more was time alone to rest and walk on the beach. Later she told me that this experience had been very interesting for her. In the past she would have wrestled with feelings of being left out or excluded because she chose not to attend the meetings and be part of the group. She would have referenced herself externally. This time she let herself do exactly what *she* wanted to do. She was referencing herself from inside. This was so new to her that she needed to talk about it.

My son, Roddy, went to public school for the first time when he entered the fourth grade; up until then he had attended an alternative school. One day he came home and asked how one gets lead poisoning. I asked why he wanted to know. He said that he had been punished in gym class that day by being forced to stand against the wall with his face in a ring. He was afraid that the ring was made of lead and that he had been poisoned.

This seemed like a rather extreme punishment to me, especially for a kid for whom a word or a look was almost always sufficient, so I marched on the school.

What I learned was that Roddy had a "problem"; he was not fitting into the regimentation of the class. (Having gone to an alternative school, he was under the mistaken impression that gym and sports were supposed to be fun and exercise and release for the body.) I firmly believe that elementary-school gym classes are among the places where children first learn to fit into a militaristic society, and I said as much to the principal. I told him that we as a family believed in nonviolence and a nonviolent, nonmilitaristic approach to education.

The principal, rather confused by now, said that he wasn't sure he understood me. "I suggest," he told me, "that you instruct your son to go along with something, even when he thinks it isn't right, and question it later."

I was horrified and said, "Absolutely not!" I did not want my son to be so out of touch with his morality that he could one day participate in a My Lai. The principal was asking me to train Roddy to switch to a external referent and ignore his internal referent.

In fact, *neither* can or should be ignored. There are times when we must use external referents. It is only when these become the primary or exclusive means of referencing ourselves that we get into trouble. For example, it is important that I take in information from those around me, yet I cannot let this information completely determine what I do. We need both, not either/or. Unfortunately, we have been so thoroughly trained in the process of the external referent that we are not even aware that an internal referent exists.

Another of my friends is a leader in alternative education; that is, education appropriate to the individual and his or her level of achievement and awareness. My friend defines himself as a rebel, one who is against the system. In doing so, he is using the system as the point of reference by which he defines himself.

But he is not actually a rebel. He is simply doing something new and different.[2] He is marching to his own drummer and doing what he believes to be right. He is trying to develop an educational process that develops internal referents *and* still considers external referents.

Consider how closely the process of the external referent is related to the Addictive System characteristic of self-centeredness. The self-centered person recognizes no bounds between the self and the other. As a result, such a person has no way to distinguish external referents from internal ones, and in fact they become the same, resulting in the loss of both the self and the other.

THE PROCESS OF INVALIDATION

Since the White Male System/Addictive System defines itself as reality, everything else is unreal by definition. Since its referent is the external referent, the internal referent is unreal and nonexistent by definition. The process of invalidating that which the system does not know, understand, cannot measure, and thereby cannot control is so extreme that large areas of perception and knowledge are lost. *We give the system the power to make the known unknown.*

Most women have had the experience of being in a group of men, saying something absolutely profound, and getting no response at all, only to hear one of the men say the same thing a few minutes later and be immediately acknowledged as brilliant. The woman (who has been made invisible or nonexistent) starts to wonder what she did wrong, or what is wrong with her, and she says little or nothing from that point on (which may be the expected, hoped-for response).

It is very important to understand the *process* that makes someone or some idea or perception nonexistent, because this is one of the most powerful processes at work within the Addictive System. A primary function of any addiction is to make ourselves and our own processes invisible to ourselves and others. Since the self and the processes of the self cannot easily be measured or controlled, they must be *defined* into nonexistence.

Whole areas of knowledge and information have been defined into nonexistence because the system cannot know, understand, control, or measure them. One of these is what I call "extravagant living," which, as I mentioned earlier, I define simply as being alive. People who are alive are harder to control. They tend to think and feel for themselves. They put the quality of their lives and the lives of others at the top of their list. For a system to gain a modicum of control over people like this, it must ensure that they develop addictions.

Rather than admitting ignorance of areas that it does not know or understand, the Addictive System makes them nonexistent, thereby obviating the problem. However, various civil rights movements, for one example, have refused to disappear, and this refusal has proved a major irritation. As minority groups have become more evident and vocal, it has become increasingly difficult to define them out of existence. And most such groups, having started realizing their identity and obtaining their validation from within, are less willing to accept nonexistence.

Another form of invalidation mentioned earlier is to find any small thing wrong with what is being said and thereby dismiss *all* that is being said.

THE PROCESS OF TRASHING/FABRICATING "PERSONALITY CONFLICTS"

Although they appear to be two different processes, trashing and fabricating personality conflicts, both have the same effect.

The process of trashing was ably discussed in *Ms.* magazine in the 1970s.[3] Basically, trashing is a process that is used against individuals to call their credibility into question. When it is successful, it renders people powerless and totally destroys their influence within a group. During the 1970s it was used quite effectively by women against other women.

The ideology of the person being trashed is never called into question. Instead, the trashers concentrate on character defamation. People being trashed are accused of being unethical, immoral, dishonest, or power-hungry, and anything they say is dismissed on the basis of that supposed weakness of character. The element of projection is often a factor. For example, people who accuse others of being power-hungry often appear to be themselves desperate for power.

There is also an attempt to isolate from the group anyone who had anything to do with the person being trashed. It becomes too costly to associate with the trashee. It takes so much energy to remain within the group and simultaneously to associate with the person being trashed that eventually the association is just not worth it.

Of course this process has little or no relationship to the value of what the trashee has to say or who the trashee is. The purpose is to render someone ineffectual, a nothing.

The same is true of the process of fabricating "personality conflicts." Several years ago I consulted with a group about their staff functioning. As I observed the staff at work in a number of situations, it became clear that one member was on a severe and prolonged "dry drunk" and was exhibiting many of the characteristics of the alcoholic. She was the source of many of the unfounded rumors within the organization; she was holding down several other jobs at the same time, and her coworkers rarely knew where she was or what she was doing. As a result the whole staff was confused and ineffectual, and she was the focal point of this confusion.

It also became obvious that the rest of the staff was supporting her behavior by choosing not to confront it. I began to deal with this issue in my consulting; after all, I was there to find out why the organization was not functioning well.

I soon began to hear rumors that this person and I had a "personality conflict." I was astounded. We had not yet interacted enough for there to be any grounds for a personality conflict. I did not dislike her, and in fact my intent was to see that she was given the opportunity to get the treatment she needed, which, I hoped, would result in the best possible service being provided to the organization's clients. But she set up the illusion of a "personality conflict" between us in order to discredit my observations of her. If we had a "personality conflict," then my observations could not be "objective"; and hence, they could not be valid.

A variation on this theme happened recently to one of my friends. She had written a book challenging some of the beliefs currently held in the field of mental health. Her perceptions were very controversial. One of my colleagues gave the book to a mental health professional who obviously had a strong personal reaction. Instead of saying, "I don't like the book," "I disagree with her perceptions," or God forbid, "I feel threatened by those ideas," he immediately tried to discredit the author by calling her a hysterical female.

This not owning one's own reactions and feelings—projecting them onto the other person in an attempt to discredit something that is threatening or that would require one to change—by discrediting the messenger is all part of this same technique of the Addictive System.

The main purpose of trashing and fabricating personality conflicts is to dismiss or invalidate the input from a particular individual. Ironically, the intensity of either process is usually directly proportional to how frightened the person initiating it is, and how true, thus powerful, the information is that is being dismissed or invalidated. In treatment circles, this behavior is called "protecting one's supply."

THE PROCESS OF DUALISM

The final process I shall discuss here is the process of dualism. If there is any process that is basic to all characteristics and processes of the Addictive System, I suspect this may be it. Almost all the characteristics I have described as being inherent to this system and all the processes I have delineated thus far can be seen to emerge out of dualistic thinking.

Most of us are trained in dualistic thinking. Our education prepares us to think dualistically—either this or that, either right or wrong, either in or out, either off or on, either black or white, either good or evil, and so on *ad infinitum.* I believe that this kind of thinking serves many functions in this system. The first is to oversimplify a very complex world, thereby giving us the illusion of control over what is in fact a universe in process. When we think we can break something that has many complex facets into two clear dimensions, it feeds our illusion of control.

The process of dualistic thinking also sets up a situation in which, if one part of the dualism is affirmed, the opposite is automatically assumed to be false. It is like the old mother-son interaction: the son says, "I like the blue shirt," and the mother responds, "What's the matter, you don't like the red one?"

In dualistic thinking, if we state that something is *right,* then the assumption is that the opposite must be *wrong.* The world is perceived as pairs of opposites. There is no recognition that both "opposites" can be right, or that there may be other alternatives besides those two. The very process of dualism prevents us from generating or considering alternatives. If white women are working for their own liberation, then they must be working *against* the liberation of women of color—an example of how dualism has been used to separate and divide women from one another. Another example is the assumption that when one disagrees with the policies of our government one then supports the enemy. In dualism there is no possibility that we can think that we are wrong *and* they are wrong also. Hence, opinions are squelched because of the process of dualism. There are many other uses of this process in this system, as we shall see.

The process of dualistic thinking also serves to set up a situation in which one feels forced to choose between two options, even when (which is often the case) neither is acceptable! This process serves to keep a person stuck and supports the illusion that stability (stasis) is possible and even desirable.

For example, I see many women in therapy who say, "Should I leave my husband or stay with him?" Usually neither option is acceptable at that point, and vacillating back and forth between them keeps the women stuck in the situation and incapable of either making a decision or considering other options. I often ask them to generate more options—an odd number like three, five, seven, or nine. When they realize that they have more than two options, they can find ways to move in and around and through (and even out of) their situation.

Dualism keeps us confused and indecisive, believing that we *must* choose between two undesirable opposites—the rock and the hard place or the frying pan and the fire.

Dualistic thinking also operates on a societal level. One must be either a Democrat or a Republican, or a Christian or a non-Christian, or a believer or an unbeliever, politically correct or politically incorrect, for busing or against it. I have a friend who is a nun. At one point she decided to live in our household. I experienced some concern about the kind of support I could give her since I was raised a Protestant. "My dear," she said jokingly, "there are no such things as Protestants. There are Catholics and non-Catholics." Self-centeredness like this is also dualistic thinking. All these forms of dualism confuse us, keep us stuck in the system, and effectively prevent change and evolution.

In the Living Process System such choices and setups are irrelevant and simply do not exist, because choices are made consistent with one's inner process, one's spirituality.

LINCOLN LOGS

A few years ago, when I started seeing how dualistic thinking affects us, I developed what I now call the Lincoln Log Theory. It has turned out to be a very nice shorthand and very exciting and useful to me. The way it works is very simple: Picture a Lincoln Log. (You know, the kind for building log cabins. Most of us played with them as children.) Now picture one part of a dualism at one end of it, and the other part at the other.

Most of the issues that emerged as I was working with people in therapy came in pairs—dualisms. The first one I became aware of in working with women was the dualism of powerlessness and control. I saw women trying to give up their controlling behavior and not being able to do it, and also trying to give up their powerlessness, equally unsuccessfully. It then became clear to me that powerlessness and control were the same Lincoln Log. They go together.

It is not possible to deal with control issues unless we are also willing to give up our feeling of powerlessness. This is something with which women in particular have considerable difficulty because we have been conditioned to feel powerless. It seems almost impossible to feel any other way, but unless we begin to own some of our personal power, and perceive that power coming from inside us, we cannot begin to let go of our need to control the world around us.

Another example is something that I have observed in women who have been incest victims as children. Frequently, they have only two methods of relating to men: They either avoid men, or they are seductive with them. They seem to bounce from one end of this Lincoln Log to the other, and both ends serve the function of avoiding intimacy. As long as these women stay on this Lincoln Log, they will never develop meaningful relationships with men. They must completely move off this dualism, let go of both behaviors, and begin to operate out of another system to become whole and have the opportunity for intimacy. They cannot just move out of being seductive or just stop avoiding relating to men. They must do both.

Another way to understand this concept is by envisioning a narrow-gauge railroad. They basically do not go anywhere. The trains run back and forth between two points, from one end to the other, over and over again.

Or think of a seesaw. At one end is one part of a dualism, and the other is at the other end. My clients would tip from powerlessness to control, and from control to powerlessness, up and down. They were unable to climb off the seesaw (or the narrow-gauge railroad, or the Lincoln Log).

I began imagining that our heads are filled with stacks of Lincoln Logs, carefully arranged one on top of the other, and like pickup sticks, one, if removed, throws the whole structure into chaos. I had many fantasies about the possibility of a sort of Lincoln Log psychosurgery that would remove the whole structure from our brains, so we could finally begin to think and perceive and act in different ways. So far, I have not perfected this surgical technique.

My discovery of the powerlessness-and-control Lincoln Log was only the start. Following are discussions of some of the others I have encountered over the past few years.

FEAR AND CONTROL/DEPENDENCY AND CONTROL

Fear and control is a Lincoln Log. We cannot give up our need to control (illusion of control) unless we are willing to relinquish our fear; we cannot give up our fear unless we stop trying to control. The two are inextricably linked. When we are fearful, we try to control. When we try to control and (invariably) fail, we become more fearful.

Dependency and control is another Lincoln Log. We cannot become ourselves without giving up the need to control; we cannot give up the need to control while we are dependent on someone or something outside us for our survival. When we are dependent, we feel as if we *must* control, because we do not have inside ourselves what we need to survive. Controlling other people, situations, and things seems the only way to get what we need.

I often see these Lincoln Logs emerging full force in couples getting a divorce. This, of course, is a fearful time for both. Their lives are changing radically. Instead of seeing their feelings of fear as normal, welcoming them and working through whatever they need to with respect to them, they become progressively controlling of themselves, their lawyers, and their ex-partners-to-be. Fear and control go together; as we understand this relationship we have more options.

SELF-CENTEREDNESS

As I said earlier, self-centeredness is one of the major defining characteristics of the Addictive System. There are many Lincoln Logs with self-centeredness at one end.

The first is the Lincoln Log of *self-centeredness and nonexistence.* As I noted earlier, one of the characteristics of self-centeredness is the total lack of boundaries between the self and others. Everything is ME. Everything happens to ME. Everything is directed for or against me (a dualism?). At the same time, we feel as if we do not exist, that we are not real. Self-Centeredness is an attempt to cope with that feeling. It is not possible to give up one without also giving up the other. One of my trainees recently said, "When I am self-centered, I am completely out of touch with myself." Now that sounded strange to me, for being self-centered seems to imply being *over*occupied with the self. Then I realized she was right!

Self-centeredness as defined in the Addictive System has nothing to do with being aware of the real self. If one has no boundaries and does not recognize others' boundaries, then there is no real self. One must give up both self-centeredness and nonexistence to have a self. Lincoln Logs are very tricky!

The second is the Lincoln Log of *self-centeredness and disrespectfulness.* When we focus only on ourselves, when we see ourselves as the defining center, when we perceive everything as being done in relation to ourselves, we have a tremendous disrespect for others. It is not possible to respect others without giving up our self-centeredness, and it is not possible to give up our self-centeredness until we start to recognize where we end and others begin, that they are not the same as we and we are not the same as they. When we do this, we see and respect ourselves and we see and respect others. As long as we remain self-centered, we will be disrespectful of others by definition.

The third is the Lincoln Log of *self-centeredness and self-negation.* When we refuse to listen to ourselves and deprive ourselves of information coming from within, we tend to become self-centered. We must focus on ourselves too much in order to be aware of ourselves at all. It is not possible to give up our self-centeredness unless we also stop ignoring ourselves, and we cannot stop ignoring ourselves unless we stop perceiving ourselves as the center of the universe, around which everything else revolves and by which everything else is defined. I often find this Lincoln Log functioning in persons who are trying to deny the self for religious reasons. While trying to be "selfless" and think only of others, they often function in a very self-centered fashion, completely oblivious to anyone around them. Such persons, for example, often do not feel that they have to follow the societal rules that others follow, because they are serving others they are therefore exempt. It is an interesting and subtle Lincoln Log.

The fourth of these is the Lincoln Log of *self-centeredness and guilt.* Guilt in and of itself is a remarkably self-centered activity. It involves a lot of "Woe is me," "Oh my goodness, what have I done?" "I feel bad," "I, I, I . . ." People focusing on their own guilt are completely unaware of those around them. It is not possible to give up feeling guilty about everything we do unless we stop believing that the world revolves around us, and it is not possible to stop believing that the world revolves around us unless we relinquish our guilt over everything that goes on in our lives.

The final Lincoln Log in this series is the one of *self-centeredness and shame*. Like guilt, shame is a very self-centered activity. When we are ashamed, it is because we believe that many other people and events are dependent on us or related to us, and we have somehow let them down. It is not possible to let go of our shame unless we abandon our self-centeredness, and it is not possible to move off our self-centeredness unless we let go of our shame. The two support each other. I believe people who are not self-centered do not experience shame.

SHAME

Shame shares a Lincoln Log with something other than self-centeredness: perfectionism. If we did not believe that it is possible to be perfect (as defined by the Addictive System), we would not be ashamed of being who and what we are, whatever that is. It is because we fail at perfection that we feel ashamed and unable to accept our nonperfection and learn from it. If we believe it is possible to be God as defined by the system, we are inherently ashamed of our humanness. Believing we can be God is the very core of self-centeredness. If we were not ashamed of ourselves, we would stop striving to be perfect. Shame and perfectionism are inextricably linked.

GREED

As I continued to unearth more Lincoln Logs, I could not help but notice how closely they are related to what we call the Seven Deadly Sins—food for thought!

Greed is another Addictive System characteristic that has several Lincoln Log partners. The first such partnership is greed and the scarcity model. Greed stems directly out of the conviction that there is not enough of anything to go around. When we believe that we must scramble for everything, we become greedy. As we feed our greed, we believe more and more that there will not be enough. It is not possible to let go of our greed without dealing with our adherence to the scarcity model, and vice versa.

The second is greed and stinginess. When we are greedy, we also tend to be stingy with others (and especially ourselves). When we are stingy, we also tend to be greedy in relation to others (and ourselves). This is a Lincoln Log I have often seen operating within the church or organizations that do not operate out of an abundance model. When that organization is stingy with what it has, it also tends to become greedy in acquiring more. We cannot let go of our stinginess without letting go of our greed; we cannot let go of our greed without letting go of our stinginess. We must abandon both at the same time, or we will continue to run from one end to the other of this Lincoln Log.

The third is greed and self-denial. A colleague recently discovered this Lincoln Log within herself. She had gone to a workshop and had taken some time off during it to pick blackberries. The more she picked, the greedier she became. At the same time, she felt guilty about taking time away from the workshop. She was in the habit of denying herself the time and freedom to pursue quiet activities (like picking blackberries), and now that she was actually doing it she could not get enough. She suddenly realized that unless she was willing to let go of her self-denial, she would not be able to let go of her greed, and unless she was willing to let go of her greed she could not deal successfully with her self-denial. If she gave herself more time in her life for blackberry picking, she probably would not believe that she had to get all her blackberries at one time.

DISHONESTY

Several Lincoln Logs have emerged in relation to dishonesty, another characteristic of the Addictive System we discussed earlier.

The first is dishonesty and niceness. I find this Lincoln Log especially prevalent in religious groups and women's groups, although men are certainly involved too. To maintain the illusion of niceness, it is often necessary to be dishonest. For example, someone asks you to do something that you really do not want to do, but you say, "Yes, of course, I don't mind, I'll do it." You agree in order to be nice, and you are dishonest because you really do not want to do it. Niceness for its own sake and dishonesty are inextricably linked. We cannot stop being dishonest unless we relinquish our image of niceness, and we cannot become genuinely caring unless we stop being dishonest. (Somehow, when we become honest, both of these seem to fall away with our doing little or nothing.)

The second is dishonesty and rightness. I have been working with a woman who has a tremendous need to be right, even when she is clearly wrong, and this need often interferes with her need to be honest. She moves into dishonesty and starts distorting facts, figures, and information to maintain her rightness even when she knows that I know the facts. Unless she is willing to let go of her rightness, she will not be able to attain the honesty she knows is important; she will have to let go of dishonesty *and* rightness to become clear and make a system shift.

We can see this same phenomenon on a system level. As a government, when we do not feel good about some of our dealings internationally, instead of admitting our error and moving on, we become dishonest and try to cover it up with dishonesty. If we were not so invested in our rightness, we would not have to be so dishonest. I think this is a good example of how what we see going on at an individual level is also occurring at the level of the system and vice versa.

Another Lincoln Log that we can see functioning on the personal and the systemic level is that of rightness and defensiveness. When it is absolutely necessary to be right (even when we know we are not), we get defensive. Often we end up defending a position that has no validity whatsoever (and is therefore indefensible). Being right becomes more important than being truthful or honest. We cannot give up our defensiveness without giving up our need to be right; we cannot give up our need to be right without giving up our defensiveness. They function together.

REPRESSION AND OBSESSION

For some time now I have been fascinated with the obsession that the church, particularly the contemporary Catholic church, seems to have with sex. For example, I have been looking at the way the church makes sex the most important aspect of the relationship between a man and a woman. I have realized that repression and obsession occupy the same Lincoln Log, and that when we repress something (like sex) we tend to become obsessed with it. If we deal with sex as a normal function and not central to and defining of all relationships, we do not spend much time thinking about it. When we mystify it and keep it secret, we become obsessed with it. We cannot deal with that obsession, let it go, and move beyond it until we also deal with our repression; we cannot deal with our repression until we are willing to leave our obsession behind.

This Lincoln Log relates to many things besides sex. For example, when we repress anger we become obsessed with it. When we repress pain we become obsessed with it. When we repress sorrow we become obsessed with it. *Anything* we repress eventually becomes an obsession unless we are willing to bring it out into the open, deal with it, and let it go.

WORTHLESSNESS

Many of the women I work with express feelings of worthlessness. Ironically, those people who profess their worthlessness most vehemently are also those who seem to perceive themselves as better than everyone else! Two more Lincoln Logs have emerged out of this awareness.

The first is worthlessness and grandiosity. Whenever people start proclaiming how worthless they are, they also (almost in the same breath) get very grandiose about who they are, what they can do, how fantastic they are, and how important they are. The two go together, and we continue to move back and forth between them unless we discard them both. One almost seems to breed the other!

The second is worthlessness and superiority. Those people who claim to feel the most worthless tend to lord it over others; those who tout their superiority have deep-seated feelings of worthlessness. For example, I had a trainee who was very intelligent and highly educated and had a Ph.D. in a prestigious field. In spite of that, he had very low self-esteem. Unfortunately, he had a pattern of being the "authority," lording it over others and, in general, exuding an air of benevolent superiority. When he was honest with himself and the group, he often stated that he felt like "a piece of shit." As he began to feel better about himself this "superior" behavior began to drop out also. He was moving off the Lincoln Log. As one characteristic disappeared, the other went with it. We cannot deal with one aspect of this Lincoln Log without also dealing with the other. To recover, the entire Lincoln Log must be removed and the person must shift to another system.

JUDGMENTALISM

Judgmentalism is integral to the Addictive System, and I have found it on two Lincoln Logs to date.

The first is judgmentalism and rigidity. People who tend to be judgmental also tend toward rigidness, rightness, and superiority. Similarly, rigidity breeds judgmentalism. When we are rigid, we cannot be flexible and "go with the flow"; when we are judgmental, we become rigid in ourselves, with ourselves, and with our way of dealing with the world. We cannot give up one without the other.

The second is judgmentalism and self-righteousness. When we feel self-righteous—as if we are totally virtuous, moral, and ethical —we become judgmental. When we are judgmental, we feel self-righteous. We cannot give up judgmentalism unless we are also willing to give up our self-righteousness.

This judgmentalism-self-righteousness Lincoln Log is often seen in the members of fundamentalist religious groups. They are continually professing the soundness of their beliefs, and it is a natural next step to judge other people and their beliefs as wrong, incorrect, or crazy. (And as long as they can judge others in this fashion, they can continue to believe that they are in the right!)

Most often this Lincoln Log has its source in insecurity. If you are not sure of yourself and your perceptions, then the support of others becomes very important to you. In *Women's Reality* I talked about this vis-à-vis Reactive Female System women: because we are so insecure about ourselves and our place in the world, we feel compelled to convince others to agree with us. We become self-righteous and adamant about our perceptions, and we become judgmental of people who do not share them because we so desperately need their support to feel good about ourselves.

Both judgmentalism and self-righteousness are counterproductive, and when they are joined they leave no avenue to open-mindedness or change.

SELF-DEPRECIATION AND ENVY

When we depreciate ourselves, when we do not value ourselves, when we do not trust our own perceptions, when we lack confidence in what we are doing with our lives, we tend to be envious of others. We compare what we are doing with what they are doing, or what we have with what they have, and we fall short in our own eyes.

Conversely, when we envy others it is almost always because we are not valuing ourselves and what we are doing. We cannot curb or let go of our envy until we stop depreciating ourselves and seeing everything we are doing as having little or no comparative value. The word comparative here is key; when we are truly focusing on what we are doing and need to be doing, there is nothing to compare with anyone else and no reason for envy.

I often find this Lincoln Log in people who are not doing their own work, whatever that may be. When we are not doing our own work, we start to wonder what everyone else is up to, and that leads to envy. But when we are paying attention to ourselves, valuing ourselves, and doing our own work, envy just does not enter in.

We cannot get rid of our envy without letting go of our self-depreciation; we cannot stop depreciating ourselves unless we leave our envy behind.

BLAME AND IRRESPONSIBILITY

When we do not take responsibility for our lives, when we do not own them and acknowledge that they are ours, when we do not incorporate and deal with them in all their aspects, then we tend to blame others for who we are (or are not). When we blame others for the shape our lives are in, we do not have the option of taking responsibility for our lives.

There is no way to deal with our past, regardless of how traumatic it was, if we refuse to own it. Unless we realize that it belongs to us (and represents opportunities for learning and awareness), and unless we assimilate it and work through whatever we need to work through in relation to it, we blame others. We see them as being responsible.

The blame-irresponsibility Lincoln Log keeps us at a distance from our own lives and the gifts of learning and insight we have received along the way. It actively prevents us from learning what we need to learn, knowing what we need to know, doing what we need to do. We cannot give up blaming others unless we take responsibility; we cannot take responsibility unless we stop blaming others.

PRICKISHNESS AND NEEDINESS

One of my friends is frequently "prickish"—hard to be around, sullen, snotty, irritable, and sending out all kinds of disturbing messages with her eyes, her body, and her speech. Whenever she is like this, people stay away, which seems to be her intent.

Sometimes I tease her about this behavior, and at one point a trainee of mine observed, "Well, after all, you have to prick a prick." Now *prick* is a term very rarely used to describe women, and yet in this particular case it seemed apt.

This remark led to the naming of the Lincoln Log of prickishness and neediness. We found that my friend got prickish whenever she was feeling needy—needing to be touched, to be held, to have someone pay attention to her. It happened most often when she was involved in a kind of Addictive System neediness, the kind that expects something *out*side to satisfy it. As we all looked at this behavior more closely, my friend became aware that she was expecting something outside to meet her needs, realizing that this expectation could not be met, and getting prickish as a result. When she began to focus on herself and her own needs and work with her neediness, her prickishness vanished.

She could not give up her prickishness until she dealt with her neediness, and she could not give up her neediness until she dealt with her prickishness. Once she recognized this Lincoln Log, she was able to let go of the whole thing.

ANALYSIS AND PARALYSIS

Another of my trainees helped to identify the Lincoln Log of analysis and paralysis. She tends to be very logical and rational and intellectual in dealing with her own issues, and as she analyzes them (and analyzes them, and analyzes them) she gets stuck and incapable of going anywhere.

As we all worked together on this awareness, it became clear that analysis leads to paralysis, and that one of the effects of paralysis is the tendency to analyze. Analysis almost never leads to resolution and action, although we fully expect that it will. When we analyze, we tend to stay stuck. The two are part of the same dualism.

We cannot "move" unless we give up being stuck, and we cannot get unstuck unless we give up analyzing why we are stuck.

FEAR AND ANGER

I have already noted that fear shares a Lincoln Log with control. It shares another with anger.

When we are fearful, we are usually angry at the same time. When we are angry, it is fear that is most often at the root of our anger—fear of ourselves, and/or fear of others. When we operate out of fear, we are almost always angry because we perceive the world as an unsafe place; when we are angry, we help to make the world an unsafe place because our anger generates retaliatory anger in others.

When we let go of our fear, our anger dissipates; when we let go of our anger, we have that much less to fear.

WIN AND LOSE

When we operate out of a mind-set that insists that we win at everything we attempt, there is always the potential for losing. When we operate out of a mind-set that convinces us that we will lose at everything we attempt, the possibility of winning still exists and goads us on. Stuck in this dualistic system, we run back and forth between win and lose, lose and win.

In a process system, winning and losing are irrelevant. Such concepts do not even exist. Win and lose belong to the Addictive System.

HOPELESSNESS AND PERFECTIONISM

Shame and perfectionism are one Lincoln Log; hopelessness and perfectionism are another.

Whenever we try to be perfect, we end up feeling hopeless, because perfection is an illusion. Whenever we are feeling hopeless, we tend to try to become more perfect in order to hook into a belief in ourselves out of our hopelessness. We teeter back and forth between the two.

We cannot give up perfectionism without also letting go of feeling hopeless about our lives; we cannot stop feeling hopeless unless we are willing to stop striving for perfection.

ARROGANCE AND GOING ONE-DOWN

In *Women's Reality* I discussed the "one-up, one-down" assumption that exists in most relationships. Basically, it says that two people cannot exist on the same level, as equals; instead, one must always be "one-up" while the other is "one-down."

When we go one-down, we tend to believe that the only way to get out of that position (and go one-up) is to be arrogant. When we are arrogant, we tend to believe that where we really belong is one-up, and therefore that everyone else must be one-down. We cannot even conceptualize the possibility of being equal with another person, or of that person being equal with us.

We must give up both our arrogance and our willingness to bide our time being the underdog; the two are part of the same Lincoln Log. It is only when we refuse to be either one-up or one-down that we can start relating to others as equals and allow them the same privilege.

CYNICISM

Cynicism is a part of at least two Lincoln Logs.

The first is cynicism and idealism. We often see this Lincoln Log at work in our interpersonal relationships; it is how some families deal with the world. They start out full of hope, believing that everything is possible and that people are essentially good. Then, as soon as something happens to mar that rosy picture, they become cynical and superior. They dismiss, devalue, and criticize anyone who does not fit their model, and they "give up."

The second is cynicism and innocence. In this Lincoln Log, innocence functions as a sort of denial: "I simply will not see the world as it is. I will pretend it isn't there. I will operate as if it isn't there. My family will operate as if it isn't there, and then we will not have to deal with it." This refusal to face the dishonesty and controlling tendencies of the Addictive System leads to cynicism and a sense of superiority: "I'm better than other people; my family is better than other people; everyone else is essentially bad."

These two Lincoln Logs are often connected to each other. We flip back and forth between cynicism and idealism, cynicism and innocence. We cannot give up our cynicism until we are willing to let go of *both* our idealism and our innocence; we can not let go of *either* our idealism or our innocence until we leave our cynicism behind.

What I see happening in the Living Process System is a movement toward a combination of innocence and wisdom. We do not have to be cynical; neither do we have to wear blinders all our lives. We can see the world as it really is and continue to be vulnerable to it.

ENABLING AND IGNORING

The Lincoln Log of enabling and ignoring is most apparent in co-dependents.

Co-dependents do not know the difference between *taking care of* and *caring for*. After long periods of taking care of other people (and enabling their dependencies), they become resentful, hostile, and drained. As a result, they start ignoring the people they have been taking care of, who then respond by demanding even more caretaking. The co-dependents then move back into taking care of them (just to shut them up!).

Co-dependents stay stuck on the Lincoln Log of either enabling and taking care of or becoming drained and ignoring. They move back and forth between the two, over and over again. Many of us had parents who parented in this way: they alternated between giving us their all and abandoning us emotionally to struggle along on our own. I think that many of the fears of abandonment found in co-dependent families are based on this Lincoln Log. We grow up believing that there are only two ways to function within a relationship: by doing everything for the other person, or by ignoring her or him completely.

We cannot truly *care for* someone without the mutual understanding that we will not abandon that person; we cannot arrive at this understanding unless we give up our enabling behaviors.

MALE AND FEMALE

The last Lincoln Log I want to discuss here is male and female. For quite some time I did not even think of it as a Lincoln Log, but the more I considered it, the clearer it became that it, too, was a process of the Addictive System.

Recently I was reading *The Further Education of Oversoul Seven* by Jane Roberts when something the character Oversoul said leaped off the page at me (to paraphrase): "Oh, yes, Earth; you're the people who believe in male and female, and the separateness of each."[4] It was then that I saw male and female as a Lincoln Log —male at one end, female at the other. But this, like all the other Lincoln Logs, is an artificial representation of our experience. Each of us has what have been defined as characteristics of *both* sexes; some people are closer to one end of the continuum and some to the other end. There are countless gradations in between.

The very concept of the male-female dualism serves to keep us stuck in the Addictive System and separate from the reality of our experience, which is that we exist on a continuum in relation to what has been termed maleness and femaleness. When we insist on being *all* male or *all* female, and on everyone else we know choosing one or the other, we deny ourselves a variety of relationships and forms of intimacy.

Many women and some men have begun to realize the necessity to be who they are, which may have nothing to do with these concepts. In doing so, they are moving toward the Living Process System.

THE POWER OF THE PROCESS

We have just explored some of the processes of the Addictive System. This exploration is not exhaustive, it is suggestive. As I stated earlier, these processes are the secret strengths of the system. They are far more powerful than either its contents or its roles.

Since we have been educated in a system that is static and focuses almost exclusively on contents, we have little knowledge of or skill with processes. This is one reason they exercise such a profound influence over us. We are not trained to recognize them; we do not know what to do about them; and we do not know how to live with them.

It is when we look closely at how these processes affect us that we begin to understand the enormity of the issue. For example, the *content* of the promise often influences us greatly, yet it is the *process* of the promise that removes us from our present and our reality. It may not even matter what the content of the promise is; its process is what moves us into addiction and addictive behaviors.

But now we have an advantage: we know these processes by name. Now we can go on to explore the *how* of addiction. How have we ended up in a system whose primary emphases are powerlessness and nonliving? How have we been reduced to denying our very life force? How has this come about?

In Part II of this book I described various characteristics of the Addictive System. These are the characteristics I learned about through my own recovery and through treating addicts and other co-dependents. In recovery circles they are often classified as "character defects" or "things" from which one must recover.

It is time to see them for what they are: *processes,* not character defects or "things." When we talk about controlling behavior, we are talking about a *process.* When we talk about stinkin' thinkin', we are talking about a *process*. The same holds true for self-centeredness, dishonesty, confusion, denial, illusions, fear, tunnel vision, frozen feelings, ethical deterioration, and so on. They are all processes. They are characteristics of an *addictive* process.[5]

Realizing where the power lies gives us the power to recover and the power to aid others in their recovery. With that insight we can *really* begin healing ourselves and the system and function as healers in the world. We can and must see that we are in an Addictive System that is sustained by an addictive process that has many offshoots and permutations. As we see this truth, we can forgive ourselves and see that an entire system is diseased and desperately needs to recover.

SEEING WHAT WE SEE, KNOWING WHAT WE KNOW
IMPLICATIONS OF WHAT IT MEANS THAT WE LIVE IN AN ADDICTIVE SYSTEM

In order to effect a shift out of the Addictive System and into the Living Process System, we must first be willing to see what we see and know what we know. Let us review and elaborate upon some of the points we have discussed thus far.

1. The Addictive System will lead to total destruction.
It has a *nonliving* orientation. It requires us to relinquish our personal identity, power, awareness, and knowledge in order to "belong." It requires us to accept the possibility that the world may be annihilated any day. This must be "stinkin' thinkin'."

The Addictive System perceives all people who are truly alive as direct threats to it. Consider what happens in most Addictive System organizations whenever new people are brought in. If they are recent high school or college graduates, they start out bright-eyed and bushy-tailed. Then what happens? They are ground down. Their energy, productivity, and readiness to set the world on fire are threatening to those who are operating within the system. So they are ground down, sat on, and forced to fit in—to give up their aliveness. The spoken goal of the organization may be productivity, profit, or service; the *uns*poken goal is usually to preserve the system and the status quo.

When we think of what it means for an entire system to be oriented toward nonliving, it is almost too much to bear. When we realize that this attitude is the orientation of the system in which we live, it is truly terrifying. When we see and know that our major policy decisions are made by people who do not understand or admit to their own addictive processes, and these decisions are made by persons whose thinking processes are the same as the distorted stinkin' thinkin' of the addict, we rightfully fear for our lives and those of our children.

Must we placidly await the destruction that is the promise of the Addictive System? I do not think so, and again, I am drawing on what I know about the treatment of addicts. It used to be believed that addicts could not begin the recovery process until they had "bottomed out." Until they had gone as far as they could in their self-destructive downward spiral, they were not ripe for recovery. (Is this concept on an individual level not unlike nuclear war on a system level?) More recently some treatment centers have been accepting addicts before they are brought to their knees, and the resulting treatment has been successful. Let us hope that the same holds true for the Addictive System.

II. The Addictive System is morally and spiritually bankrupt.
I never thought much about the seven deadly sins until I began learning about the Addictive System. Now I see and know that these are inherent to that system and actively work to perpetuate it. I do not, however, believe that they are inherent to human beings. Pride, covetousness, lust, anger, gluttony, envy, and sloth —the sins that are traditionally deemed fatal to spiritual progress —are woven, as we have seen, into the very fabric of the Addictive System. (Interestingly, they are also seen as character defects in the treatment of the addict. They must be worked through for the

addict to begin the recovery process.) We can see how the drunk or addict will do anything for a fix. What does this obsession mean on a system level?

What besides covetousness and gluttony pushes companies to manufacture drugs of questionable healing value and then sell them to the public? What causes these same companies to remove them from our stores' shelves when they are past the expiration date, repackage them, and market them to Third-World countries where they have caused illness and death?

What besides gluttony moves trainers to drug horses so they feel no pain when they run on injured muscles and bones? What causes them to claim on television that they "did it for the good of the animals"?

We are inured to the moral and spiritual bankruptcy we see and know all around us. We have become so accustomed to the flagrant lying of our public officials that we no longer have the skills we need to discern dishonesty from truth. As I said earlier, I believe that these skills reside not in the rational mind but in the solar plexus; a "gut feeling" tells us when we are being lied to. But how can we receive messages from our built-in lie-detection center when we numb it with alcohol, drugs, food, gambling, money making, and workaholism?

We live in a system in which it is no longer safe to leave our children in the care of "nice old ladies" because some "nice old ladies" use them as the objects of their own and other's lust.

We live in a system that exploits the bodies of women, children, and men to sell products. We live in a system that sets up increasingly elaborate and complex agencies to control and regulate dishonesty—agencies that time and again prove dishonest themselves. We live in a system in which we find excuses to overlook and explain the lies of our political leaders—just as any co-dependent in an addictive family would do.

We live in a world that is literally turned upside down by moral deterioration. It has redefined morality to fit its behavior. It has made its behavior the norm and defined it as morality.

I know of at least one religious community whose leader is a practicing alcoholic. He often appears in public drunk. The whole community functions as an addictive family in excusing his behavior (some even say it is part of his teaching of the imperfection of the human being!), and in doing so every member exhibits the symptoms of co-dependence. The whole community coalesces, makes excuses for its leader's drunkenness, and supports the continuation of his illness—which is no favor to him.

The addictive process is so insidious, and dishonesty and denial are so integral to it, that it is difficult to see and know that our system is morally and spiritually bankrupt. The system itself is its own disguise. Add to this the fact that living in it robs us of the clarity to recognize it for what it is, and things become even more confusing. (Recall that confusion is one of the defining characteristics of the Addictive System.) Please remember that to say the system is sick is not to say it is bad. The only hope for recovery comes from confronting and naming the disease.

III. The Addictive System is wrong about the human condition.
About three years ago I spoke at a seminar on some of the concepts introduced in *Women's Reality.* We had just been discussing the White Male System myth that it is possible to be God as defined by that system when one of the women in the audience spoke up.

"I am not sure that this is a myth of the White Male System," she said. "I think that it may just be the human condition to want to be God."

The day before I had returned from a visit to the Hawaiian Islands, where I had spent some time learning about the Hawaiian people and their customs. I knew that they had never wanted to be God (at least, not until the missionaries arrived). That information was enough to convince me that it was *not* the *real* human condition to want to be God: it was the human condition as defined and understood by the Addictive System.

I began to wonder how much else of what we had been taught was equally skewed to fit the system. Was our entire understanding of who and what we are based on the perceptions of the Addictive System?

Then I started thinking about the church, the source of our theological learning. Was it not true that it, too, was part of the Addictive System and worked to perpetuate it?

Gradually I came to realize that the addictive processes of the promise, absorption, control, the external referent, invalidation, and dualism are all characteristic processes of the church. It was then fairly easy to see how the church actively inhibits and interferes with our ability to approach our own spirituality. Because of its complicity with an addictive society, it, like the co-dependent, cannot do what it wants to do and compromises its morality.

The church holds forth the promise of healing and spiritual growth, but neither is possible to achieve through addictive processes. The basic truths of the church are essential to the human soul, and the vehicles of their dissemination are the vehicles of the Addictive System and by definition can only lead to nonliving. It is sad that an institution with "life and life more abundant" to give chooses a process for delivery that denies life itself.

Another institution dear to my heart that has made the same mistake is the field of psychotherapy. Psychotherapy is supposed to offer healing to the personality and the being; that is its *raison d'être*. But by utilizing techniques and processes of the Addictive System, it *is* the Addictive System, a fact it fails to recognize.

Psychotherapy has become increasingly dishonest and controlling, and because of this it cannot meet human needs no matter how hard it tries. The assumption is that the therapist must maintain control over the client at all times. It is assumed that the therapist or the technique is the actual healer. Furthermore, psychotherapy, like so many of the helping professions, has made little attempt to learn fully about addictions and addictive processes. Most therapy students are given only a single unit on addictions in their graduate training; this token instruction only feeds our arrogance about how much we know about addictions and convinces us that we do not really need to learn any more.

Any therapist who is not actively recovering from the Addictive System is perpetuating it. Any therapist who is not actively trying to make a system shift is supporting the Addictive System.

Psychotherapy makes yet another mistake by treating disorders in isolation, out of the context of the Addictive System. For example, there has been a great deal of interest in narcissism in some therapeutic circles. Well and good; narcissism is certainly an interesting concept, and as a paradigm it explains a cluster of behaviors. It is also essentially the same as self-centeredness, which is something that the professionals who treat addicts know a lot about. Were therapists to acknowledge that narcissism and self-centeredness are the same, far more treatment possibilities would be available to them.

Consider also the treatment of psychoses, particularly manic-depressive psychosis. Interestingly enough, since lithium was introduced as a treatment for this disorder, there has been a significant increase in the number of people diagnosed as having it.

I once had a client who was on large doses of lithium when he came to me. I had noticed before then that the mood swings of the manic-depressive were very similar to the mood swings of the alcoholic, and we decided, with the cooperation of my client's physician, to base our therapeutic approach on this discovery. We decreased and eventually terminated his use of lithium, and this approach worked out just fine. Meanwhile we began treating his addictions.

We worked through his first addiction of choice (marijuana) and his second (alcohol), and he proceeded through his recovery. Afterward we tackled his addictions to nicotine, sugar, and food (he is severely hypoglycemic). Then we started in on addictive relationships, sex, and money.

What had initially been diagnosed as manic-depressive psychosis turned out to be a clustering of addictions. Seeing and knowing this made it possible to treat his addictive process *and* the specific addictions.

I am not implying that *all* psychological illness can be attributed to the Addictive System; I am saying that ignorance of the Addictive System can perpetuate *any* such illness, and the illness may, indeed, be an outgrowth of living in an Addictive System.

IV. The Addictive System is wrong about human development.

As I stated earlier, we have been taught that adolescent rebellion is a normal stage in human development. We have been taught that the whole purpose of adolescent rebellion is to separate oneself from one's parents and establish one's own identity. But what if an adolescent is parented by someone who is *not* controlling, dishonest, self-centered, and dependent—in other words, *not* part of the Addictive System? Would such an adolescent then have to pull so far away?

If adolescents were raised to be in touch with their feelings, to act out of them, and to respect the feelings of others, would they really need to alienate themselves from their parents? Or would their identities develop gradually all by themselves? If adolescents grew up knowing themselves, would they have to rebel?

I see this concept of adolescent rebellion as only one of many that merit reopening and rediscovering. Everything we know about human development has been taught by Addictive System teachers in Addictive System schools from a perspective of a "reality" that is not real. These are just some implications of these ideas. As we discover more, we have a better chance to move toward recovery as a total system.

SUMMARY

When I first became aware that the White Male System and the Addictive System are one and the same, I felt completely overwhelmed with elation. It happened while I was speaking at a wellness conference. The words tumbled out of my mouth, a hush fell over the audience, and then there was a spontaneous standing ovation.

It is always a tremendous relief to name the truth, no matter what it is. As a famous teacher once said, "Ye shall know the truth, and the truth shall make you free."

One reason that I was so overwhelmed by this awareness was my own experience with what a lengthy and difficult process recovery is. It can take from two to five years for the addict to begin functioning in any consistently clear way, and the co-dependent at least that long. This is the minimum time required when people are genuinely working and wanting to get well and actively doing the things that are necessary to move along in that process.

How long might it take for a whole system to recover? And what if that system doesn't even know it is addictive and lacks a collective desire to get well?

Another concept that had been difficult for me to accept was the AA notion that one is always recover*ing* from an addiction or addictions and never fully recover*ed;* that recovery itself is a process and never an accomplished fact. How could a system that is so goal-oriented ever accept that concept? Yet, I knew that that very goal orientation was itself indicative of the Addictive System. Did this mean that we could not look forward to a time when our system would recover?

And how could we initiate the process of recovery? Intervention with an individual is hard enough, and it can take all one's energy just to break through the denial that a problem exists. I knew that part of the definition of an addiction is that it has hold of the person, not vice versa. Denial is the means by which that hold continues. When the system around us supports and is part of that denial, how could we ever penetrate it on a systemwide basis?

Finally, what we have named as reality is an Addictive System, and the nature of that system is not to see reality. How could we break through that?

Where could we begin?

Thus far, this has been a book descriptive of the system in which we live. I have been working on the concept of a Living Process

System for over twenty years and for the past five years, I have been conducting year-long training programs in that system. My forthcoming book, *Living in Process,* will describe that system and how it functions in detail. However, I want to close with some ideas that point in that direction.

IV. TOWARD RECOVERY AND HEALING

WHOLE-SYSTEM RECOVERY

Can a whole system recover from its addictions? The idea is staggering. Yet alcoholism is one of the few fatal diseases for which the possibility of recovery is guaranteed. Why not recovery for a whole Addictive System?

During the last presidential campaign I watched several television programs relating to the election. I noticed a renewed interest in the gender gap, due partly, of course, to Geraldine Ferraro's being nominated for the vice presidency and partly to emerging statistics. The gender gap appears to be widening, and Americans are increasingly approaching basic issues from a gender-related perspective. The more I listened to the men and women being interviewed, the more astonished I was to see them taking up positions along distinct Addictive System and Living Process System lines.

For example, in general the men interviewed seemed to feel that peace could be achieved only through control and intimidation, whereas the women interviewed seemed to feel that it could best be achieved through negotiation and understanding. When couples were interviewed, wives and husbands differed sharply in their opinions.

We are beginning to *name* those differences system-wide, and often they have clear correlations with gender. This is not to say that men are not concerned about the same issues as women; they are. But in general women are articulating them differently at this point.

THE ROLE OF NAMING

I began this book with a discussion of the importance of naming. I now return to that idea, which I see as key to understanding the

Addictive System and beginning the process of recovery for the whole system.

We cannot recover from an addiction unless we first admit that we have it. Naming our reality is essential to recovery. Unless we admit that we are indeed functioning in an addictive process in an Addictive System, we shall never have the option of recovery. Once we name something, we own it. Once we own it, it becomes ours, as does the power we formerly relinquished to it. Once we reclaim that personal power, we can begin to recover and not until then. Remember, to name the system as addict is not to condemn it: it is to offer it the possibility of recovery.

Paradoxically, the only way to reclaim our personal power is by admitting our powerlessness. The first part of Step One of the AA Twelve-Step Program reads, "We admitted we were powerless over alcohol." It is important to recognize that admitting to powerlessness over an addiction is not the same as admitting powerlessness as a person. In fact, it can be very power-full to recognize the futility of the illusion of control.

The second part of Step One is an admission "that our lives had become unmanageable" (which they are—in relation to the addictive process). If we fail to see this unmanageability, we continue to try to control the addiction, a goal impossible to achieve. It is only when we *name* our situation that we become ready and able to do something about it.

It is possible to see the Twelve Steps operating on a systems level. I believe that one reason the program is so effective in the treatment of addicts is that it confronts and deals with the addictive process in a process way in addition to a particular addiction or addictions.

When I first became aware of the Twelve-Step Program, I was very skeptical and had a hard time keeping an open mind. I now see why: at that point in time, I was firmly entrenched in the Addictive System as a co-dependent. I voiced the usual arguments: "The Twelve-Step Program becomes an addiction in itself . . . AA takes over one's life and becomes a be-all and end-all—social group, church, family . . . many of the people who attend AA

meetings don't look all that healthy . . . too many of them smoke
. . ." I did not want to accept that recovery was a *process* and that
one had to go to meetings and work the program for the rest of
one's life. It was too much!

Then one day I realized that working the program was very
much like breathing for me. I breathe all the time, and I never
complain about it. I do not get up in the morning and say, "Oh,
darn, I have to breathe again today." I live on a planet with a
certain atmosphere, and in a certain kind of body, and therefore
I must breathe to stay alive, so I do.

I began to see this as analogous to living in an Addictive System.
I have chosen to continue to live in this system, so I must do the
things that will keep me alive from day to day. I must take time
to be alone. I must take care of my spiritual needs. I must think
and reflect. I must check myself out for symptoms of backsliding
into addictive behaviors and do whatever is necessary to return to
clarity—or sobriety, as the Twelve-Step Program calls it. In other
words, following the program for me is just like breathing. I no
longer resent it. In fact, I recommend that all my trainees try
working with some sort of Twelve-Step Program as an aid in
making a systems shift.

As I travel around the country, I am amazed at how many people
are actively involved in a Twelve-Step Program as the result of one
addiction or another. In a way, this is a great cosmic joke. The
Addictive System encourages addictions to keep people so far
away from their feelings and awareness that they cannot challenge
the system. Unfortunately (or fortunately), more and more people
whose lives are being destroyed by addictions are starting to seek
help. They are aligning themselves with recovery groups and
starting to recover. The further along they get in their recovery,
the less able they are to support and participate in the Addictive
System.

In other words, in many ways that system contains within itself
the seeds of its own destruction. This is the great cosmic joke and,
to me, a hopeful sign.

THE ADDICTIVE PROCESS: CLOSING NOTES

There is much more to say about the Addictive System and the addictive process, and much more to discover. As we near the end of this book, I have a few additional thoughts and comments, and some ideas I want to review and reiterate.

On the dry drunk: The concept of the dry drunk, as taught by AA, is very useful to understanding the addictive process.

Everyone who works with alcoholics knows that recovery means more (much more) than just giving up the chemical. A person can be dry for days, months, even years, and still not be sober. Someone who quits drinking and continues to evidence the characteristics and processes of the addiction is termed a dry drunk. Achieving sobriety takes time *and work.* Recovery is a process.

A dry drunk is someone who is not recovering from the addictive process. A co-dependent, who may never have touched a drop of alcohol, is someone who is not recovering from the addictive process. The diseases of addiction and co-dependence are the same, and they function in precisely the same ways. The alcoholic may turn to alcohol and the co-dependent may turn to food, but the dynamic processes of their addictions are the same. Each is dishonest, controlling, and self-centered.

We have been so focused on the *content* of addictions—as one would expect, given our Addictive System point of view—that we have neglected to develop the tools we need to hone in on the addictive process and what it means.

We can see the dry drunk working on a system level. Individuals who are not chemically dependent and yet function in the addictive process are on a dry drunk. Organizations that make assumptions out of the addictive process based on such processes as dishonesty, manipulation, control, and confusion are on a dry drunk. Educational and political systems that function on Addictive System assumptions of control and dishonesty are on a dry drunk. Here we have the hologram at all levels. The dry drunk syndrome is functioning the same as the individual on a dry drunk and vice versa. There is no difference.

On ingestive/process addictions: One of my friends has made some fascinating observations about ingestive and process addictions. She points out that of the two, process addictions always have the wider social component.

Ingestive addictions affect us on a personal level, making it more comfortable for us to live in the Addictive System and making us more suitable for that system. Process addictions, on the other hand, have more far-reaching effects: they cause us to lose our moral and social perspective on a global scale and to participate in destroying far more than ourselves and our immediate environment. The process-addicted people are the builders of bombs, the proponents of apartheid, the makers of the Dalkon shield.

On the Addictive System being a closed system: As I said earlier, the Addictive System is a closed system. It is a system that turns back on itself in a convoluted way and becomes more and more enmeshed in itself. This book not only describes that process, it is written in that way. As we read about the characteristics *and* the processes, we can see how dishonesty leads to confusion, which leads to control, which leads to dishonesty, and on and on. Everything I have described in this book convolutes and turns back on itself. That is how the Addictive System operates. Nothing is distinct and clear. It is all convoluted and unclear. This is one way the system has perpetuated itself. It is not possible to grab a piece and deal with it. It is like Freud's theories: They operate as a closed system. Anyone who disagrees is functioning out of defense mechanisms and, hence, cannot be trusted.

I am aware that in this book I have repeated myself and used one idea to illustrate another. That is how a closed system operates. It is confusing *and* it is the system in which we live.

On three perilous processes: There are three processes that seem to plunge us back into the Addictive System whenever we practice them. I have discussed each at length and want to emphasize them again here. They are *dualism, dishonesty,* and *control.*

Whenever we succumb to any of these three, we are immediately back into behaving addictively. Whenever we think dualistically or are dishonest or controlling, we may as well have "taken a drink." The effects lead us to a dry drunk, and we must then move to reestablish our recovery process. All other characteristics and processes of the Addictive System seem to flow naturally out of these three.

On the Addictive System as point of reference: As we treat the addictive process within ourselves and start recovering from it, we literally begin to do life differently.

One of the major differences is that we no longer use the Addictive System as a point of reference. We do not go along with it, but we do not fight it, either; it simply has no more relevance to us. It is no longer our point of reference. It is meaningless, remote, inconsequential. We are completely separate from it. In making a systems shift, we have left it behind.

PARADIGM SHIFT/SYSTEMS SHIFT

In *The Aquarian Conspiracy*, Marilyn Ferguson frequently notes that we are living in a time of paradigm shift.[1] I have come to believe that this concept is itself tied to a static, nonprocess system. If we were living in a true process system, we would probably just evolve new ideas!

The notion of paradigm shift is based on the buildup of information and the subsequent, drastic introduction of new information. It involves being wrenched out of where we are and forced to go somewhere else.

Although I perceive this concept differently from the way Ferguson does, I still find it very useful. She claims that we are now in the process of a paradigm shift, and that it is widespread throughout our society at the grass-roots level. She has documented her theory well, yet I do not really believe that the attempts she has documented will succeed unless the element of addiction is recognized and dealt with.

I think that what she is perceiving is a shift into the Living Process System that will render the Addictive System irrelevant. The popularity of twelve-step programs and other recovery programs for addictions are indicative that such a shift is going on. These are some of the tools we have needed for a long time, the tools we can use to facilitate a systems shift. There are others that are emerging, such as spirituality and meditation. We need them all.

THE HOLOGRAM IN ACTION

The holographic concept I introduced earlier is that the individual is like the system and the system is like the individual. As people start shifting into a process system that is free of addictions and addictive behaviors, the system itself is making a similar shift. As the system changes to support that shift, individuals have still more options for change.

The part is like the whole, the whole is like the part, and in some very basic ways they are the same. Changes in one are changes in the other and are reflected in both directions. What an exciting possibility!

SOBRIETY, PROCESS, AND SPIRITUALITY

I believe that *sobriety, process,* and *spirituality* are all words for the same process.

When individuals embark on recovering from chemical addictions, they are told that their sobriety must be the most important thing in the world to them or they will not recover. Putting their sobriety first does not mean that they have to leave their mate, their job, or any other relationship or situation in which they are involved; it does mean that they have to be *willing* to leave should that relationship or situation threaten their sobriety. Nothing can be allowed to come between them and their sobriety, for if they do not achieve sobriety they will die.

I think that we can equate our spirituality and our process with sobriety. We cannot allow anything to come between us and our spirituality, or between us and our living process. If we do, we shall destroy ourselves and those around us.

There is an image I share with my trainees that I will use here in closing.

I imagine the universe as an enormous puzzle. Each of us is a unique and vital piece of that puzzle. No one else has our genes, our life experience; no one is *us*. We are unique! When we are fully ourselves we are that piece.

In an Addictive System, we are trained *not* to be ourselves. We lose touch with ourselves. We reference ourselves externally. We deny who we are. This leaves a hole in the puzzle and a hole in the universe that no one else can fill.

Because we have been living in a system that is an addictive system, we are living in a universe that has many holes. As we begin to claim our lives, our pasts, and our selves, that hole in the universe is filled.

It is in living our own process that we take our place in the universe and the whole system can then heal.

Notes

Part I: The Addictive System

1. *How Democracies Perish* (Garden City, NY: Doubleday); Morris Berman, *The Reenchantment of the World* (New York: Bantam, 1984); Masanobu Sokuoka, *The One Straw Revolution* (Emmaus, Pa.: Rodale Press, 1978); Fritjof Capra, *Turning Point* (New York: Simon & Schuster, 1982); Jay D. Fast, *Entropy* (New York: Gordon, 1978); John Naisbitt, *Megatrends: Ten New Directions Transforming Our Lives* (New York: Warner Books, 1982); Elizabeth Dodson Gray, *Green Paradise Lost* (Wellesley, Mass.: Roundtable Press, 1982).
2. Anne Wilson Schaef, *Women's Reality: An Emerging Female System in a White Male Society* (Minneapolis: Winston, 1985).
3. Ursula LeGuin, *The Wizard of Earthsea* (New York: Bantam, 1974).
4. Tillie Olsen, *Silences* (New York: Delacorte Press/Seymour Lawrence, 1978).
5. Marilyn Ferguson, *The Aquarian Conspiracy: Personal and Social Transformation in the 1980s* (Los Angeles: J. P. Tarcher, 1980). The concept of a paradigm shift was first set forth by Thomas Kuhn in *The Structure of Scientific Revolutions* (Chicago: University of Chicago Press, 1970). Kuhn states that whenever we make a scientific observation we develop a paradigm, or model, to explain it; as our knowledge about and experience with whatever we are observing increases, that paradigm becomes obsolete and we move on to another. According to Ferguson, this process is occurring throughout our system at this point in time.
6. Sharon Wegscheider-Cruse, "Co-Dependency: The Therapeutic Void," in *Co-Dependency: An Emerging Issue* (Pompano Beach, FL: Health Communications, 1984),1.
7. Charles Whitfield, M.D., "Co-Dependency: An Emerging Problem Among Professionals," in *Co-Dependency: An Emerging Issue* (Pompano Beach, FL: Health Communications, 1984), 45
8. Earnie Larson, *Basics of Co-Dependency* (Brooklyn Park, MN: E. Larsen Enterprises, 1983).
9. For a more comprehensive discussion of this topic, see my book *Co-dependence: Misunderstood, Mistreated* (Minneapolis: Winston, 1985).
10. Workshop on Adult Children of Alcoholics with Sharon Wegscheider-Cruse and Rokelle Lerner, Rocky Mountain Council on Alcoholism, Denver, Colo., January 1984.
11. Ibid.

Part II: The Addictive System as a Holographic Concept

1. Ken Wilbur, *The Holographic Paradigm and Other Paradoxes: Leading Edge of Science* (Boulder, Colo.: Shambala, 1982).

2. William Sloane Coffin, *The Courage To Love* (San Francisco: Harper & Row, 1982), pp. 49–50.
3. Many other writers have described the dependency aspect of relationships in our culture—*The Cinderella Complex* (Colette Dauling), *The Peter Pan Syndrome* and *The Wendy Dilemma* (both by Dan Kiley), *Sweet Suffering* (Natalie Shainess), *Women Who Love Too Much* (Robin Norwood), *Smart Women, Foolish Choices* (Connell Cowan and Melvyn Kinder), to name a few. However, they just have not put it together with the Addictive System.
4. Richard Bach, *Illusions* (New York: Delacorte, 1977).

Part III: Processes of the Addictive System

1. "Our Town, 1985," *The New York Times,* 21 October 1984.
2. See how even the words *new* and *different* reference themselves to the Addictive System. This is an excellent example of how language of the system supports the process of the external referent. We must think very creatively to avoid this trap!
3. Joreen, "Trashing: The Dark Side of Sisterhood," *Ms.,* April 1976.
4. Jane Roberts, *The Further Education of Oversoul Seven* (Washington, D.C.: P. H. Associates, 1979).
5. In *Co-Dependence: Misunderstood, Mistreated,* I named the addictive process as the main process of the Addictive System. The processes named in this chapter are all subprocesses of the overriding addictive process of the Addictive System. It is not surprising that we are so entrenched in these processes when they are all around, when they infuse our world and we are told that they are reality. We must recognize them for what they are.

Part IV: Toward Recovery and Healing

1. Ferguson, *The Aquarian Conspiracy.*